First Fruits
of PRAYER

First Fruits
of PRAYER

*A Forty-Day Journey
Through the
Canon of St. Andrew*

FREDERICA MATHEWES~GREEN

PARACLETE PRESS
BREWSTER, MASSACHUSETTS

First Fruits of Prayer

2006   First Printing

© 2006 by Frederica Mathewes-Green

ISBN 1-55725-469-9

Library of Congress Cataloging–in–Publication Data
Mathewes-Green, Frederica.
First fruits of prayer: a forty-day journey through the Canon of St. Andrew / Frederica Mathewes-Green.
    p. cm.
  Includes bibliographical references (p. 377) and index.
  ISBN 1-55725-469-9
    1. Andrew of Crete, Saint, ca. 660-740. Megas Kanåon 2. Spiritual life—Orthodox Eastern Church. 3. Repentance—Orthodox Eastern Church. 4. Devotional exercises. I. Andrew of Crete, Saint, ca. 660-740. Megas Kanåon. English. 2006. II. Title.
  BX375.A6M38 2006
  264'.019013—dc22

                                        2005023957

10 9 8 7 6 5 4 3 2 1

Published by Paraclete Press
Brewster, Massachusetts
www.paracletepress.com
Printed in the United States of America

To Bishop Kallistos Ware of Diokleia,
with gratitude.

Contents

vii

Introduction

What is the Canon of St. Andrew?

The Great Canon of St. Andrew of Crete is a prayerful hymn of epic length, which is offered in a Lenten worship service every year in the Eastern Orthodox Church. It was written by St. Andrew, a leading figure of early Christian hymnography. He was born in Damascus, spent his early years as a monk in Jerusalem, then went to serve orphans and the elderly in Constantinople. Eventually he was made bishop of Crete, and died in 740 AD.

St. Andrew built up his Canon from a very close examination of the Scriptures, primarily the Old Testament. As he considered each passage he took to heart the events and characters there, looking for lessons for his own life and urging himself to love God more completely. The work is very personal in tone, and St. Andrew may have written it for his own private use. As it became known throughout the Church it was taken up broadly, and has been used during every Lent since in the Eastern Church.

The Canon is not a mere historical curiosity, however. Many contemporary Christians have the sense that believers in the early centuries had a different experience of the faith than we customarily do today—more intense, more rich, and frankly, more challenging. The key was the kind of rigorous self-examination St. Andrew shows us here: a whole-hearted embrace of repentance as a path to self-knowledge and healing, and eventually to union with God. We are not used to thinking of repentance as a positive tool anymore, or as something that would continue to accompany a Christian throughout a lifetime. As we walk alongside St. Andrew, and see him search the Scriptures, and hear his humility matched by grateful confidence in God's compassion, we begin to glimpse the healing power of repentance.

How Should I Use This Book?

The Great Canon is divided into nine sections, or canticles. But for purposes of this book it has been rearranged into forty readings, one for each day of a self-directed retreat. Lent, of course, is an ideal time to enter this spiritual resource, but it could be used any time you want to deepen and challenge your faith.

Each reading is accompanied by a verse-by-verse commentary that will provide the Scriptures cited by St. Andrew and further explore the meaning of the passage. This running commentary, headed "Explore," is found on the page facing the corresponding passage of the Canon.

In each chapter, following the passage of the Canon and the "Explore" commentary, you will find a few paragraphs headed "Consider." These brief meditations will provide further thoughts about the themes raised in that day's reading, and provide questions to stir up deeper reflection.

If you have wished you could pray like the Desert Fathers did, or read Scripture like the church fathers did, or know God like the early martyrs did, the Great Canon can be a doorway. It can take you back in time to the early centuries of Christian worship, and open the way to a prayerfulness that is not bound by time at all.

The Spiritual Background of the Canon

THINGS CHANGED. The Lord Jesus Christ, who calls people to Himself today as He has for thousands of years, never changes. But the encounter with Him that we sense in our hearts is met by things we learn from the outside—information gained from Scriptures and pastors and teachers of the faith. There are also general expectations that prevail in our worshiping community, as well as some expectations of the larger society about what religious faith is and does.

Put it all together and, even though we and the earliest Christians share a common Lord, we have built up different structures around that central experience.

To start with just that word *experience*—today when we talk about "religious experience" we usually mean "emotions." On a recent TV series, a discussion panel including people of various faiths as well as atheists and agnostics assumed in common that talk about God splits in two directions, either into rational intellectual assertions ("mind") or emotions ("heart"). But early Christians expected to experience Christ in the flat, primary sense, like "I went to the dentist and experienced getting a tooth pulled." You may have thoughts and emotions about getting a tooth pulled, but the experience itself is basic.

The experience of the presence of Christ is just that real. Yet the current expectation, which unfortunately many Christians agree with, is that it's all about emotions. That's one example of how foundational assumptions have changed.

As time passed, Christians of Europe and the West separated from those in the rest of the world: the Middle

East, Africa, India, Eastern Europe, and Asia. The faith
changed more in the West, because Eastern Christians had
no mechanism for change (like a papacy and magisterium
or, later, original-thinking theologians and Reformers).
Eastern Christians also kept using the earliest forms of
worship, a custom which is itself a powerful preservative.
When Eastern Christians look westward today, what
they see (whether Roman Catholic, Episcopalian, or
Assemblies of God) has a strong family resemblance.
They perceive something that's hard for us to grasp, that
all forms of Western Christianity share the same underlying
concepts, which grew up and developed some time after
the historic split. All versions of Western Christianity
appear to be sides of the same prism.

Thus, when viewed through the grid of Western Christian
assumptions, the Canon of St. Andrew looks quite different
than it would to an Eastern Christian worshiper, whether
in the eighth century or today. Let's take a moment to get
oriented to this alternate point of view.

THEOSIS. In Western theology, the word *salvation* immediately
raises an image of the crucified Christ. His death on the
cross reunited us with God the Father, paying Him the
debt for our sins. Christians of St. Andrew's world
would have seen things from a slightly different angle.
For them, salvation is being restored to the image and
likeness of God. It means God dwelling within us and filling us with His presence.

Now, sometimes we say this in Western Christianity,
but I think we don't mean it as literally as they did. For
them, God's presence in us is like the fire in the Burning

Bush. It gradually takes us over, so that although we remain fully ourselves, we are being made over into our *true* selves, the way God originally intended us to be. He is Light, and we are filled with His light—maybe even literally, as some saints were said to visibly glow. The term for this transformation is fairly scandalizing: *theosis*, which means being transformed into God, divinized or deified. Of course we do not become little mini-gods with our own universes. We never lose our own identity, but we are filled with God like a sponge is filled with water.

This is the reason Christ came. *Theosis* is the goal of life for every human being. This belief began to be stated very early in the Church. St. Irenaeus (d. 202 AD) and St. Athanasius (d. 373 AD) kept expressing it in variations of this statement: "God became man so that man might become god."

Theosis is a biblical idea, too. When St. Paul talked about being "in Christ," or Christ being "in me," he meant it literally. That's how his words were understood by people who lived in his world and spoke his language, the ones who were his original audience.

SIN. As we are filled with this presence, we naturally shed the compulsion to sin. External acts of sin are important, but the real concern is with the inner person, with the murky depths of impulse, selfishness, and greed that we can hardly bear to face. Jesus spoke of a bad tree bearing bad fruit, and a good tree bearing good fruit. He chastised the Pharisees for being virtuous externally, but inside being like rotting corpses.

Thus we find great concern among early Christians with the "hidden person of the heart" (1 Peter 3:4). Temptation provokes desire which gives birth to sin (James 1:15), so it is necessary to guard even one's thoughts, as Christ taught when warning against lust or murder "in the heart." As St. Paul said, "take every thought captive to obey Christ" (2 Corinthians 10:5).

In fact, the Greek word for repentance, *metanoia*, means "a transformation of the mind." Repentance doesn't mean feeling bad about yourself, guilty and miserable. It is seeing the truth: admitting the truth about your sinful self, and the truth about God, which is that He already knew this truth about you and loves you anyway. He is like the father of the prodigal son; He only wants us to come home. But we are so tied up with fear and pride that it is hard to admit how much we sin, or how deep the roots go, stretching down into that darkness within. This life is a process of continual *metanoia*, mental transformation, as we keep allowing more of our sickness to come to the light and be healed. St. Paul wrote, "Be transformed by the renewal of your mind" (Romans 12:2). St. Andrew's Canon is designed to be an aid to staying on point, continually exploring repentance.

SICKNESS. It's sometimes said that we live in a "therapeutic" culture, which means that people are led to cultivate feelings of self-pity and to seek out comfort. Early Christian spirituality was therapeutic, too, but to a very different effect. Here the idea is that sin is a kind of sickness. When Adam and Eve disobeyed God, they broke the connection they had with the only source of Light and Life. They began to die. The result is that every human is born with a spiritual "broken gene," so to speak, which will inevitably dispose them to sin as well. We see the world in distorted ways. We react erratically and selfishly. Even those we love, we don't love very well. It is very lonely on this earth; we are all like miniature spacemen in our separate spacesuits, fearful and grabby and dying day by day.

The goal of life in Christ is to be healed. We apply self-discipline to curb our overt sins, then to curb our more subtle and elusive sin-patterns of thought. Gradually we acquire "the mind of Christ" (1 Corinthians 2:16). We develop His mind, literally. All these things that we tend to think of as metaphoric turn out to be literal. The wages of sin really *is* death. Sin severs the cord of connection with God, and so we die. Christ really *is* Life. When His life grows within us, we are healed and restored.

This is a really long process. It takes a lifetime. But it is God's plan for reclaiming and transforming His world. He doesn't so much act vaguely "in history," but in individual lives. Each person who is being taken over by His Spirit is a lamp in the darkness. Our responsibility is to surrender ourselves to Him entirely and be taken over by His light, which will in turn reach others.

So this isn't a private ticket to heaven. Though we may do many things to increase our self-control (like fast, keep a schedule of daily prayer, tithe, and sacrifice time and money), one of the main things God uses for our spiritual growth is other people. As they interact with us, frustrate and annoy us, we are over and over given opportunities to act in love. The main evidence that we are growing in Christ is not exhilarating prayer experiences, but steadily increasing humble love for other people.

The cardinal rule is humility. We don't understand humility very well in our culture; we're more attracted to a model of heroism, which deals out punishment to wrongdoers and wins admiration as a champion of the right. But this was not a usual feature of early Christian spirituality. Instead, even wrongdoers were to be treated with love, in the awareness that we are equally sinners. St. Paul's statement that "I am the foremost of sinners" (1 Timothy 1:15) was enthusiastically adopted, and you will see it recur throughout the Canon. Tax-collectors were pretty obnoxious people—traitors who skimmed money off the poor and served the oppressive Roman state. Yet Christ loved even them. So the goal is to avoid judging anyone, and steadfastly to resist getting angry (no fudging with a pretense of "righteous" anger; we're not righteous enough for that). Other people rub off our rough edges, and so we grow into the likeness of Christ, who forgave His enemies from the cross.

THE EVIL ONE. Every day Christians pray "deliver us from evil," not knowing that the Greek original reads, "the evil," that is, "the evil one." The New Testament Scriptures are full of references to the malice of the devil, but we generally overlook them. I think this is because our idea of salvation is that Christ died on the cross to pay His Father the debt for our sins. The whole drama takes place between Him and the Father, and there's no role for the evil one.

But for the early Christians, and as we will see in the Canon, the evil one was a very real and malevolent presence. Temptation coaxes us toward sin, and sin leads to sickness and death, and ultimately confinement in the realm of the evil one. The devil's main purpose is not to scare us, in a horror-movie way; when we're scared of him we're alert to him, and that might undermine his plans. Instead, he wants to quietly, subtly lure us into stepping away from God. Sin leads to death, but death also leads to sin. Hebrews 2:14 explains that the evil one has always controlled the human race through fear of death; death is what most deeply terrifies us and makes us grab at earthly security. But "whoever would save his life will lose it" (Matthew 16:25). That's the bitter trick. Desperate selfish clutching at life lands us in the realm of death.

But God sent Christ to rescue us; He took on human form (showing us that these humble human bodies can bear the presence of God, like the Burning Bush bore His fire), lived a sinless life, went into the realm of Hades like all human flesh, and then blasted it open by His power. Death could not contain Him, because He is Life. When we join ourselves to Him and begin to assimilate His Life, we too are freed from the control of the evil one.

This is not a "ransom" paid to the Father; the Father wasn't holding us captive. It is an offering, but not a payment. Look at it this way. Christ suffered to save us from our sins in the same way a fireman suffers burns and wounds to save a child from a burning home. He may dedicate this courageous act as an offering to the Fire Chief he loves and admires. He may do it to redeem the child from the malice of the arsonist who started the fire. But his suffering isn't paid *to* anyone, in the sense of making a bargain. Likewise, God redeemed His people from the hand of Pharaoh when He rescued them in the Red Sea. But He didn't *pay* Pharaoh anything. He Himself was not paid anything. It was a rescue action, not a business transaction, and our redemption by Christ is the same.

WHAT'S MISSING? There are some things that developed in Western Christianity that don't appear in this account at all. As you can see, there's no concept that our sins put us in God's debt legally: No idea that somebody has to pay something before He can forgive us. He just forgives us. When the prodigal son came home, the father was already running toward him with his arms open. He didn't say, "I'd like to take you back, son, but my hands are tied. Who's going to pay this Visa bill?"

This means that something else is missing—guilt. Now, of course we are responsible for our sins, and guilty in that sense. But we're not born carrying the debt of guilt for Adam's sin. That's what the fifth-century theologian Augustine of Hippo meant by the term "Original Sin." But his theory was not widely accepted in the early church (in fact, not all Eastern Christians call him a saint, and he was far from the towering figure that he became in Western thinking later on.) The idea of inborn debt compelled Augustine to say that, logically, a baby who died before baptism would have to be damned.

Instead, although early Christian spiritual writings are continually focusing on sin and repentance, the concepts of guilt and debt rarely appear. St. Andrew, like most writers of his era, views sin instead as a self-inflicted wound. Likewise, he sees God as compassionate rather than wrathful. God is always described as rushing to meet us like the father of the prodigal, or coming like the good Samaritan to bind up our wounds.

In both Orthodoxy and in the Canon, there is less of an emphasis on discrete, external acts of sin, and more a sense of it being a pervading sickness. Christ didn't come to save us just from the penalty for our sins, from death and eternal misery. He came to save us from our sins, now, today—from the poison that flows in our veins, that alienates us from the Light, that marches us toward death. He saves us like the fireman carrying that child from a burning building. We are as helpless as that child; nothing we do saves us. But as we gradually creak open the doors of our hearts we begin to discover the faint sense of His presence. He was there all along, as He is present in every person He creates. Attending to that flickering flame, we nurture it and allow it to spread, until we are filled with His light and glory.

WHY MONASTICISM? Imagine that you are at a lively party and someone asks you a question. It is an important question; your life and your future depend upon it. You would probably immediately squeeze your eyes shut and try to concentrate. You would say, "It's too noisy in here," and try to find a room where you could be alone and quiet, so you can think about how you will respond.

That is the impetus for monasticism. A monk is a person who has heard God asking him, as He asks each of us, a very important question. The surrounding world is too noisy for him to concentrate. There are the distractions of pleasure and worry that inevitably accompany everyday life in the world. There are also the interior distractions—the inner landscape of a person, involving his psychology, memories, and spiritual struggles. All this cacophony makes it hard to concentrate on the question God has posed.

The monk withdraws so that he can get away from the noise outside, so that the noise inside can begin to settle down, and he can focus all his attention on the voice of God. He begins to discern the familiar pattern of his own interior chaos, and bit by bit begins to master and subdue it. As the inner storm subsides he sees the light of Christ more clearly.

He may then return to the world in service, better fitted for it than he would have been before he mastered his competitiveness, pride, fear, lust, or despair. St. Andrew, for example, managed an orphanage and a home for the elderly in Constantinople, and served "in the world" in other effective ways till the end of his life.

Some monks remain in the monastery, but welcome visitors who come to them for guidance. Their work is somewhat like that of a psychologist, but much more broad, guiding a person's entire healing—physical, psychological, and spiritual. They are called "spiritual fathers" or "spiritual mothers," and their intense, prayerful compassion sometimes gives birth to miraculous gifts of insight ("soul-reading"). The character of Fr. Zosima, in Dostoyevsky's *The Brothers Karamazov*, is a fine portrait of the ideal spiritual father.

And some monks remain in the wilderness praying. As their own cleansing progresses, their labor of intercession becomes more and more comprehensive. They pray ceaselessly for the entire world. Miracles and healings are not uncommon, even today. (An engaging recent account is *The Mountain of Silence* by Kyriacos Markides, Doubleday 2001.)

The main charge contemporary Christians bring against monasticism is that it looks like people are wasting their lives. What good is a person who spends all his life alone in the desert? The world has so many needs. Shouldn't he be serving God there?

Of course, he may be serving God in the world in ways we can't comprehend, even by his fierce prayer on a mountaintop. But the chief problem with this objection is that it presumes people are tools. We only exist so God can get work out of us; He wants to use us like screwdrivers and crowbars to get things done in the dust of this earth.

What we find in Scripture, however, is that God *loves* us. We are the destination point of His love. That love is meant to envelop and fill us and transform us. And that's enough. If He sends us into the world, it is mostly so we can help others encounter this end-point love. We shouldn't use others as tools. God doesn't use us as tools. His goal is not a tidy world, but healed and transformed people.

This is why we hear Jesus say, "The poor you will always have with you" (John. 12:8). The world will always see poverty and pain. But even someone who is poor or disabled or mentally damaged can see God. His love knows no boundaries. Of course, when we are filled with His love we do whatever we can to alleviate suffering. But the goal of His love is not a fixed-up, repainted "Clubhouse Earth." The destination point is the individual human heart. Each one is precious, and each one needs transfiguration.

THE SHAPE OF EARLY MONASTICISM. Monastic life in the Holy Land 1700 years ago was not like the kind we're familiar with today. Contemporary monasticism seems, first and foremost, like an institution—a formal establishment with longstanding traditions, which a person enters after choosing the variety that seems best to him. But ancient monasticism was simpler, and began with a young man or woman uncovering a burning desire to live a life radically consecrated to God. She might do this by merely withdrawing to a room in her parents' house and giving all her time to reading the Scriptures and praying. She would sacrifice sleep in order to pray, and undertake strenuous fasts.

She would also dedicate herself to perpetual celibacy. When we read these ancient documents, we get the impression that Christians of the time experienced the fast from sexual relations as a powerful and energizing source of spiritual cleansing, akin to fasting from food. Food and sex are undoubtedly good, and blessed by God. But voluntarily resisting the body's innate yearnings, and continually redirecting them into hunger for God, has a powerfully focusing effect. The Greek word *ascesis*, from which we get "ascetic," means training for a vocation, or for an athletic event or challenge.

We get a feel for this in St. Paul's exhortations to "press on toward the goal" (Philippians 3:14), to "fight the good fight" (1 Timothy 6:12), and to be like "an athlete [who] exercises self-control in all things" (1 Corinthians 9:25). It's clear that this kind of self-discipline is not self-punishment, not any more than an athlete's training is. Asceticism is a galvanizing direction of the whole self in pursuit of a transfigured life. Monks are explorers on the high mountains of communion with God.

You can see how a young man or woman could be seized by such a call. The first monastics were hermits, like St. Antony; later, they lived in close communities where all things were shared (a *coenobium*), or in an in-between arrangement, where solitary cells were loosely grouped together (a *lavra*). The life of a hermit is prone to many dangers, including demonic attack and insanity; a *lavra* provided a good training ground for those who hoped to undertake that demanding *ascesis* of prayer in utter solitude.

Monastics would fast not only from sex but from meat, and often from other foods as well. Many would challenge themselves to continually reduce their diet in both variety and quantity. Each monastic needed a spiritual mother or father who could provide close personal guidance, who could exhort those who shirk duties due to laziness, or exaggerate them for the sake of showy pride, or abandon them in despair. Living peaceably in community was itself a strenuous discipline, and the early writings are full of reminders to forsake anger and judgmentalism. It was common to refrain from eating until sunset, and common to rise for hours of prayer in the night. When not at prayer monastics labored, tending a garden or weaving baskets to sell for the support of the community. Though the life was very hard it must have been purifying, because often these ancient saints are said to have lived to be ninety or a hundred.

Keep in mind that the "ascetic struggle" was aimed more at the present than the past. It was not a morbid attempt to punish oneself in order to pay for sins, or an expression of loathing for the body. The goal was to subdue "the flesh" (those selfish, death-dealing impulses, which have both physical and mental sources), while honoring "the body" (the temple of the Holy Spirit, which is made to bear the light of Christ). Thus the goal of asceticism was to be a spiritual athlete, in whom all the desires of body and mind have been purified, simplified, and united around the indwelling presence of God. Then the whole being could be radiant with the Holy Spirit, as a lantern is illuminated by a flame.

The monastic life was not an alternate form of Christian life, but an amplified one. Ordinary citizens living in neighboring towns aspired to similar rules of fasting and prayer, though they were inevitably limited by demands of daily life. The monastery stood as a center of spiritual power that overflowed for their blessing. We can make an analogy to a modern-day health club; ordinary people would visit to be encouraged in their similar efforts, to be inspired by the achievements of the great athletes, and to receive prayers and advice from these more experienced in the way. The illuminated lives of monastics gave light to all Christian brothers and sisters.

These heroic disciplines were meant to stretch and strengthen, not break, the Christian athlete. The Desert Father and revered abbot St. Poemen was asked what to do when a monk was dozing at the late service: nudge him and wake him up? "For my part," said St. Poemen, "when I see a brother who is dozing, I put his head on my knees and let him rest."

THE SCANDAL OF SAINTS. A final thing we should note, that you may find startling, is that during the course of the Canon there are occasional prayers addressed to members of the community who are no longer alive in the flesh. There are *troparia* to St. Mary of Egypt, the Virgin Mary, the Apostles, even St. Andrew himself. These *troparia* praise these saints for their courageous lives and service to the love for God, and ask them to pray for us. But how can we, and why should we, talk to them if they're dead?

For the early Christians, the most important thing about Jesus Christ was that He overcame death. He "abolished death and brought life and immortality to light through the gospel" (2 Timothy 1:10). As we saw above, death is the outcome of sin; in a bitter paradox, it is the outcome of the selfish desperation that seizes us when we scramble to escape death. Jesus Christ, by becoming a human being, showed that our human bodies and awareness could be bearers of the presence of God. By going into the realm of hades and destroying it, He showed that "death has no dominion over Him" (Romans 6:9), and when we share in His life we are likewise eternally freed from death.

This means that St. Mary of Egypt, the Virgin Mary, the Apostles, and St. Andrew are *still alive*. The early Christians would have expected that, when we begin to pray, we enter the realm of eternal, ceaseless prayer inhabited by those who have departed and now live in Christ. The heavenly realm would open to the earthly and merge with it; or, rather, the heavenly realm, which permeates the earthly at all times, would simply become more perceptible to earthly worshipers. As they stood on the floor of a humble church moving through the verses of this hymn, they would be surrounded by angels and saints, praying alongside them invisibly. (Sometimes visibly; I've heard dozens of such stories, from ordinary people who never expected such a thing. Angels have been seen in my own church.)

So it seems natural to turn to these fellow worshipers, who are privileged to stand in the unveiled presence of God, and say "Pray for me!" We ask for their prayers, just as we might ask for the prayers of a friend, a pastor, a prayer partner. A typical passage in the Canon might begin by considering the accomplishments of the Apostles, their courage, their mighty witness for the Lord. As we consider how they knew the Lord in the flesh and heard His words and touched Him, how they were filled by the Holy Spirit, how they suffered as witnesses for God, we go on to imagine their place now in the heavenly kingdom. They are washed in God's unveiled glory—and they are our friends! They are worshiping God alongside us, and we can ask them to pray for us, just as we might ask any friend. Emboldened by such thoughts, we ask them to intercede for us.

Many Western Christians are confused by such prayers to the saints, because they think it means *worship* of the saints. Instead, such prayers grow from an affirmation of the Resurrection. They are alive in the presence of God, so they are standing alongside us in worship. But we do not turn to worship them. That would be blasphemy. Instead we ask them, as our older brothers and sisters in the faith, to help us grow in Christ, and to uphold us with their prayers.

The Historic Background of the Canon

Mosaic

A shovel, then a trowel, then at last a brush: archeologists kneel on the pebbly surface of an ancient mosaic floor and uncover it to the sun, stone by stone. As the dust is brushed away a message is gradually revealed. Words are strung in a circle around the spacious floor, the words of a prayer. Once more freed from the cloaking dust of centuries, the stones cry out to God for mercy.

This dig, four miles south of Gaza City, is the site of an ancient Christian monastery. St. Hilarion was born near here about the year 293 AD, and while attending school in Alexandria made a visit to that pioneer of monasticism, St. Antony. The great man must have made a strong impression; when St. Hilarion returned home after his parents' death, though he was only fifteen, he immediately gave all his inheritance to the poor and built a hut of reeds between the marsh and the sea. There he began to live a life of intense fasting and prayer.

News got out about St. Hilarion, and people came in search of prayer for healing. Miracles resulted, and the young man's fame spread. In St. Jerome's biography of St. Hilarion, the lists of healings and exorcisms go on for page after page. But not everyone who came was seeking a miracle; some sought to emulate St. Hilarion's close walk with God. It's estimated that over his lifetime some 400 people came to live and pray under his spiritual direction. Prayer communities began to spring up in the surrounding area, and the monastic way of life spread throughout Syria and Palestine.

The site being unearthed at Tal Umm Amer is believed to be that of St. Hilarion's first monastery, built perhaps in 330 AD. The archeologists are Muslims. In an interview with the *London Telegraph*, the co-director of the project, Yasser Matar, says, "This is our history; this is our civilization and we want our people to know about it. First we were Christians and later we became Muslims. These people were our forefathers." The reporter notes that as he says this, "a burst of gunfire—echoing the region's troubles—sounded in the distance."

A few miles away, at Nusseirat, another dig is under way. This monastery was built around St. Hilarion's burial place, sometime after 370 AD. Here the mosaics are in brilliant reds, greens, blues, and ocher yellows, and show animals, birds, fountains, and flowers. Ahmed Adelrahman, director of the excavation, hopes eventually to develop a museum at the site. "There are no tourists now, but they will be back one day," he told the Agence France-Presse, as an F-16 warplane streaked across the sky.

Where Did the Christians Go?

In the New Testament we see the followers of Jesus in Jerusalem, on the hill of Calvary and in the upper room on Pentecost, and then going into all the world to preach the gospel. But not all of them left the Holy Land, of course. Then as today, a church sends out missionaries, but not every member of the church packs up and leaves town. Some of them stayed behind, near the places where Jesus walked and taught, the land of their ancestors. Some of them were descendants of people we read about in the Gospels—children and grandchildren of Zaccheus, Martha, and Photini, the woman at the well. Some of them are still there.

The book of Acts shows us a few more glimpses of Christian life in Jerusalem—there's the first church council, convened by St. James, in Acts 15—but after that we lose the thread, and our attention shifts to Europe and Rome. It's natural that we're most interested in our own backyard. But Christians continued to live in Jerusalem, and they faced a catastrophe almost immediately, when Romans besieged and then destroyed the city in 70 AD. A member of the community had been warned in a dream, and the Christians fled to safety at Pella. They returned to a field of rubble where there was "not one stone upon another," as Christ had warned (Matthew 24:2). Yet they continued to live near the sites of Christ's earthly life and their own heritage, and there as elsewhere they were persecuted by the occupying Romans. The conquerors noticed that the outlawed sect was drawn to a hillside outside the city walls, a place where criminals were tortured to death, and where there were tombs. In order to discourage them, they leveled it and planted a temple to Aphrodite there.

When the Emperor Constantine declared tolerance for the Christian faith in 313 AD, the persecutions ended. The Emperor's mother, St. Helena, went on pilgrimage to the Holy Land, seeking the places where Jesus lived and walked. Christians in the city were able to show her the place of the empty tomb, now hidden under Aphrodite's temple. St. Helena had the site excavated, and discovered in the pit remnants of three crosses, one of which proved to have miraculous powers. She had a fittingly beautiful church built on the restored site, which she called "The Church of the Holy Sepulchre" in remembrance of Christ's victory over death.

It was a period of flowering faith. Across the Holy Land many Christian institutions and churches were built to the glory of God, including the monasteries built by St. Hilarion and others. But the region lies in the path of powerful nations, and has always been vulnerable to invading armies. St. Helena's church was destroyed by Persians and rebuilt on a more modest scale; of the original structure only a mosaic floor remains. Then Muslims laid siege to Jerusalem, and after long resistance it became clear that the starving community could no longer survive. In 638 AD, St. Sophronius, the patriarch of Jerusalem, went out in great sorrow to the Muslim camp and surrendered the city to the conqueror, *'Umar ibn al-Khattab.* We will meet St. Sophronius again.

St. Andrew

Come forward now a few decades after the Muslim conquest of Jerusalem. Another young man is entering the monastic life. He has come from his birthplace in Damascus to the monastery called Mar Saba, which is set into the wall of the Kidron Valley that winds east from Jerusalem toward the Jordan River. (*Mar Saba* is Aramaic for "Lord Saba;" St. Saba established his hermitage here in 478 AD, and the monastery has been continually occupied ever since. Even today, across the valley from the communal monastery, a visitor can see the caves once occupied by solitary monks. Perhaps one day the call of God will fill them again.)

St. Andrew was born in Damascus to a devout Christian family, but caused them much worry because, at the age of seven, he had never spoken a word. According to the story, one day they took him to church and he received Communion, and from then on began to speak fluently. It seems that with this awakening he acquired an intoxicating love both for God and for words, a combination that would equip him to write out his love of God in hymns and poetry of such compelling beauty that they have been treasured by every succeeding generation.

At St. Saba he quickly won the admiration of his companions. In some ways his story is the familiar one of a wunderkind, a brilliant young man whose gifts rocket him to fame at an early age. But, to us, an "early age" is thirty. We expect everyone, even the most gifted, to incubate for a few decades before stepping out on stage. When St. Andrew appeared at the Mar Saba monastery, in 675 AD, he was fourteen or fifteen. Little more than a decade later he would hold a significant post at the most important church in the world. (People started younger in those days.)

St. Andrew impressed the community at Mar Saba not only by his eloquence, but by his spiritual purity. He showed a meek and gentle spirit toward others, while displaying heroic self-control in his own prayer and fasting. After a short time he moved to Jerusalem itself, and was attached as a monk to the Church of the Holy Sepulchre. His gifts soon singled him out for appointment as *notarius*, or secretary, to the patriarch of the city. (In the ancient Christian world there were five patriarchal cities: Jerusalem,

Antioch, Rome, Alexandria, and Constantinople. While Jerusalem had unequalled spiritual significance, it was never a large or powerful city in the worldly sense.)

When the Sixth Ecumenical Council was called in 680 AD, St. Andrew was sent to Constantinople as a representative of the patriarch, who remained with his people in occupied Jerusalem. Once again, St. Andrew's eloquence impressed his hearers, and soon he was invited to take up a position as archdeacon at Constantinople's most brilliant church, Hagia Sophia. (The name translates "Holy Wisdom," and honors Christ as the Wisdom of God.) As a deacon, St. Andrew was active in caring for the poor, and managed both an orphanage and a home for the elderly.

At the close of the century St. Andrew was made archbishop of the city of Gortyna, the capital of the island of Crete. The Muslim conquest had continued to spread around the Mediterranean basin, and the citizens of Crete had been attacked and enslaved only a short time before. Those woes were compounded by bitter controversy within the Church: a heretical view that Christ had no human will, but only the will of God ("one-will" theology, or "monothelitism") made a reappearance, even though it had been condemned at the Sixth Ecumenical Council, which St. Andrew attended as a youth. In 712 AD we find St. Andrew attending a monothelite synod, apparently under duress, an event for which he was later pardoned.

The Great Canon

In spite of, or perhaps inspired by, these miseries, St. Andrew began to produce his most glorious works. The Church has preserved some forty of his sermons and discourses, but he is most honored for his hymns, and in particular for devising a new form of hymn called a canon.

As a young monk, St. Andrew would have heard every day, at the matins service, the nine Biblical Canticles. (They're sometimes also called Odes, or Songs.) These very rich passages of Scripture praise God for His work in history for our salvation. Since these Canticles will keep making appearances throughout the Great Canon, let's take a moment to examine them. The Biblical Canticles are:

1. The First Song of Moses, Exodus 15:1–18
("I will sing unto the LORD for he has triumphed gloriously.")

2. The Second Song of Moses, Deuteronomy 32:1–43
("Give ear, O heavens, and I will speak.")

3. The Song of Hannah, 1 Samuel 2:1–10
("My heart exults in the LORD.")

4. The Song of Habbakuk, Habbakuk 3:2–19
("O LORD, I have heard the report of Thee.")

5. The Song of Isaiah, Isaiah 26:9–21
("My soul yearns for Thee in the night.")

6. The Song of Jonah, Jonah 2:2–9
("I called to the LORD, out of my distress.")

7. The First Song of the Three Young Men, Septuagint Daniel 3:26–56
("Blessed art Thou, O LORD.")

8. The Second Song of the Three Young Men, Septuagint Daniel 3:57–88
("Bless the LORD, all ye works of the LORD.")

9. The Song of the Virgin Mary, Luke 1:46–55 ("My soul doth magnify the Lord," in Latin called the *Magnificat*) combined with the Song of Zacharias, Luke 1:68–79 ("Blessed be the Lord God of Israel," in Latin called the *Benedictus*.)

I'd better take a moment to explain what "Septuagint Daniel" means, in number 7 and 8. The Septuagint is a translation of the Hebrew Scriptures into Greek, made by Jewish scholars around 250 BC. It is said that there were seventy of these scholars, which is where the name "Septuagint" comes from. These scholars made the translation because so many Jews were living abroad and no longer spoke Hebrew; even in the Holy Land, the language was becoming archaic, largely replaced by Aramaic. Greek was chosen because it was the common commercial language of the age, much like English is today.

The Septuagint is older than any existing Hebrew version of the Old Testament. When New Testament writers quoted the Old Testament, they nearly always used the Septuagint. This was the Bible of the early church, and is the version used by St. Andrew.

In 90 AD, a Jewish council voted to delete some sections of the Septuagint, declaring them non-biblical. Christians had been using the Septuagint in theological debates with Jews, and found the new Hebrew version less friendly (for example, the Septuagint Isaiah 7:14 reference to "a virgin will conceive" was rendered in Hebrew as "a young woman will conceive.") Christians ignored the Jewish decision and continued to treat the Septuagint as their version of the Old Testament Scriptures. However, when Martin Luther made his translation in the sixteenth century, he deleted the same passages the Jewish council had, so they do not appear in Protestant bibles. These passages continue to be included in Orthodox and Roman Catholic Bibles.

Back to St. Andrew: as he encountered these Canticles over and over every day, he began to weave his own prayers around them. Eventually he was composing canticles of his own, and a simple phrase from a Canticle could be enough to inspire a whole realm of contemplation. A common theme could then be explored through a series of nine Canticles which, taken together, make up a canon.

Repentance is the theme in the Great Canon, but that is the theme of virtually all Christian writing in the early centuries. That is, no matter where you look, in liturgical, evangelical, biographical, devotional writing, you find Christians exploring the dynamic balance between two interdependent truths: We are helplessly ensnared in sin, and God, in boundless compassion, rushes to rescue us. The more we trust His love, the more we are able to repent; the more we repent, the more powerfully we experience His love. Repentance is joy. This isn't a common idea in contemporary Christianity, but as you encounter it over and over again in writings like the Great Canon, it begins to fall into place.

In the Canon, St. Andrew presents the example of multi-tudes of characters from both Old and New Testaments, to call the mind to self-awareness. The first verse of each canticle, called the *irmos*, refers to the Biblical Canticle that it corresponds to. For example, the First Biblical Canticle is

Moses' song of triumph as he sees Pharaoh's hosts drowned in the red sea. He sings, "The LORD is my strength and song, and he has become my protection." The *irmos* of the First Canticle of the Great Canon begins, "He is for me unto salvation Helper and Protector."

But there's something else about these initial verses (plural, *irmoi*) that we can't catch in English. Each one establishes a particular metrical pattern, and is sung to a particular melody. The melody suits the words and embodies them expressively, in a way that can't really be translated. Every subsequent verse (called a *troparion*) in a canticle will follow the pattern and melody of the *irmos*, and then the next canticle will begin with a new *irmos* and a new pattern to follow. This elaborate structure is impressive in the original; sometimes it included additional fancy foot-work, such as acrostics. But in English, these *irmoi* and *troparia* don't look like much more than short prose paragraphs.

St. Andrew wrote a number of canons, but it appears that the Great Canon came at the end of his life, since there are several references to his old age. Those who heard it found it immediately appealing, and it began to be used in public worship in Jerusalem and Constantinople even during his lifetime.

The Canon is "Great" because it is magnificent, but also because it is so long, running to some 250 *troparia*. (For purposes of this book I have numbered each verse, including repetitions and additional prayers to saints and apostles, so the total is higher.) In the first week of Lent it is offered on the first four nights, a quarter of it each night. But it is in the fifth week of Lent that the entire Canon is offered as one. All worshipers stand as much as they are able, as is traditional in Eastern Christian worship, to show honor to the presence of the King. After each *troparion* of the Canon worshipers repeat, "Have mercy on me, O God, have mercy on me." While saying this they make the sign of the cross over themselves and bow to touch the floor (a gesture called a *Metania*), or even make a full prostration, kneeling and touching the floor with their foreheads. These worshipers do this well over two hundred times.

St. Mary of Egypt

The annual service of the Great Canon also includes a reading of the Life of St. Mary of Egypt, another treasure from the ancient spiritual writings of the Holy Land. St. Mary of Egypt was a female hermit who died about 522 AD. The gripping story of her life, and her encounter with a very surprised monk on a solitary Lenten retreat, was preserved in a monastery near the Jordan. When St. Sophronius became patriarch of Jerusalem, he heard the story and wrote it down

St. Sophronius was a prolific writer and hymnographer who was born in Damascus about the year 560 AD. In mid-life he accompanied St. John Moschus on a pilgrimage to visit the hermitages and monasteries of the Middle East, and the compilation of stories this journey produced became the classic known as *The Spiritual Meadow*. The prayers he wrote for the service of the Great Blessing of the Waters, on the feast of Theophany (Epiphany), are among the most gloriously exultant of the church year.

St. Sophronius, in his capacity as patriarch of Jerusalem, had the unhappy task of surrendering the starving city to

Muslim conquerors, in 638 AD. He died soon after, it is said, from grief.

When St. Andrew arrived in Jerusalem several decades later he encountered this story of St. Mary, and took it with him to Constantinople when he attended the Sixth Ecumenical Council in 680 AD. From there its popularity began to spread. St. Mary's life presents a vividly encouraging example of the possibility of profound repentance, even for the most desolate and degraded life. It shows how the healing power of repentance can cultivate purity of heart, transforming a person into a bearer of Christ's light, enabling him or her to do the very works He did. Best of all, it reminds us that it is all right for this to take a very long time. God is patient. St. Mary embodies the beatitude, "Blessed are the pure in heart, for they shall see God." Her story forms an excellent background to the Canon, and several passages in it ask for her prayers.

Since the story of St. Mary of Egypt is closely linked to the service of the Great Canon I wanted to include it here, but the original account by St. Sophronius is quite long. Instead of reprinting it, I have paraphrased and summarized, but (I hope) without adding to or changing the content. I recommend the original, which can be readily found on the Internet.

This story is read on the evening that the Great Canon of St. Andrew is offered. The first half, roughly to the point that St. Mary begins to tell Zosimas her story, is read before the first canticle; the remainder is read before the fourth canticle.

With all these elements—the prayer service that frames the evening, the life of St. Mary of Egypt, the very lengthy Great Canon, and the repeated responses and *metanias*—

this evening's service can take over four hours. Worshipers have arrived at the fifth week of Lent, which means they have been keeping a demanding and uninterrupted fast (essentially, a vegan diet) for over a month. The church is dark, lit only by a few candles. The smoke of incense rises and disappears in the dim heights. There are no bells on the censer; it is mute. At the chanters' stand a few worshipers take turns chanting through the canticles. Other worshipers stand here and there throughout the nave, gazing at the faces of Christ and of the saints on the icons, closing their eyes in silent reflection, and continually repeating the humble refrain of "Have mercy on me" as they cross themselves and bow to the ground.

The experience is both extremely demanding and indescribably transporting; it is like nothing else you can experience in worship. It makes an indelible impression, and as the opportunity to experience this worship returns each spring, the heart quickens with anticipation.

Stepping into the Prayer

We are ready to begin the Canon of St. Andrew. Yet as you begin you will have a sense that it has already been going on a long time, as if you are joining something already in progress. As you go through the "Explore" section of commentary, take the time to look up the Scriptures in your own Bibles and discover their meaning in context. The Canon does not naturally divide into forty readings; I have done so for the sake of this book, but the divisions are necessarily somewhat arbitrary. (The verse numbers are also my own, and don't appear in the original.) So keep in mind that, each day, you are partaking of a little bit of a continuous experience. You may not come to a tidy conclusion at the end of each reading, as you would in a book of separately composed meditations. The Canon may initially seem somewhat repetitive, but that very repetition is what enables it to write itself so deeply in your consciousness. You may have already read a number of books about early Christian spirituality: This book takes you to the next step, as you begin to practice it.

Remember to keep your attention suspended and expectant, focused on the Lord. Allow yourself to worship through the prayer of St. Andrew and through the prayers of so many Christians over all these centuries, and let this hymn soak into your bones.

The
Canon
of St. Andrew

CHAPTER 1

EXPLORE

1.   The first troparion, or *irmos*, of Canticle One echoes the first of the biblical canticles, the Song of Moses:

> "The LORD is my strength and my song, and he has become my salvation.
> This is my God, and I will praise him, my father's God, and I will exalt him" (Exodus 15:1–19).

The first Christians understood Christ's resurrection in exactly these terms. We were enslaved to sin and death and in the grip of the evil one, who desires only our destruction. Christ came and, taking on our nature, lived and died as one of us. In profound humility, He suffered in the flesh. But once inside the realm of death, He smashed it by His power. He is "the Author of Life" (Acts 3:15) and so "it was not possible for him to be held by [death]" (Acts 2:24). Our salvation is a rescue action, like this mighty one by the Red Sea.

2.   **"Where shall I begin to weep?"** The very next troparion strikes a sudden contrast. We were exulting in our salvation, but now a voice is heard weeping. How can we participate in this great salvation? What **"first fruit"** can we offer? God in compassion offers forgiveness; how can we prepare to receive it?

The whole self, both the **"wretched soul"** and the flesh, must make confession and strive for change.

3.   **"Offer to God tears."** There is much in the Fathers about weeping over sin, and it is meant literally. The ability to weep in repentance was regarded as a gift from God, something that stony, selfish hearts could not achieve. This is not a convulsive, emotional kind of weeping, however, which could be self-indulgent. It is a gentle flow of tears that is, paradoxically, freeing and consoling. This gift of tears was prized among the Desert Fathers. It was said of Abba Arsenius, who had once been a Roman senator, that, although he was still a noble and handsome figure, "Through much weeping his eyelashes had fallen out."

4.   **"I have rivaled in transgression Adam."** (Genesis 3:1–19) The Fall of Adam and Eve.

CHAPTER 1

CANTICLE ONE

1. He is for me unto salvation Helper and Protector. He is
my God and I glorify Him, God of my fathers is He and
I exalt Him, for He is greatly glorified.

   Have mercy on me, O God, have mercy on me.

2. Where shall I begin to weep for the actions of my
wretched life? What first-fruit shall I offer, O Christ, in
this my lamentation? But in Thy compassion grant me
forgiveness of sins.

   Have mercy on me, O God, have mercy on me.

3. Come, wretched soul, with thy flesh to the Creator of all.
Make confession to Him, and abstain henceforth from
thy past brutishness; and offer to God tears of repentance.

   Have mercy on me, O God, have mercy on me.

4. I have rivaled in transgression Adam, the first-formed
man, and I have found myself stripped naked of God,
of the eternal Kingdom and its joy, because of my sins.

   Have mercy on me, O God, have mercy on me.

3

5. **"The first Eve."** (Genesis 3:6, Eve takes the fruit.)
   "Wast grievously wounded." Sin is not seen so much as a bad deed meriting punishment, but rather as a self-inflicted wound.

6. **"Instead of the visible Eve, I have the Eve of the mind."** This is a striking phrase. The real source of sin is the mind. "[E]ach person is tempted when he is lured and enticed by his own desire. Then desire when it has conceived gives birth to sin; and sin when it is full-grown brings forth death" (James 1:14-15). **"Passionate thought"** makes sin appear sweet, but it is revealed as bitter.

7. **"Adam was banished."** (Genesis 3:23)
   "Always rejecting Thy words." (Acts 7:39) "Our fathers refused to obey [Moses], but thrust him aside, and in their hearts they turned to Egypt."

8. **"Guilt of Cain's murder."** (Genesis 4:8, Cain kills Abel.)
   St. Andrew says that, in annihilating and despising his own conscience, he has committed a kind of murder. He has killed his sensitivity to the subtle voice of God, a murder which will guarantee his own death in sin. The free choice of sin is a kind of suicide.

9. **"Abel in his righteousness."** (Genesis 4:4, Abel's acceptable offerings)

10. **"Cain . . . offered . . . defiled actions."** (Genesis 4:5, Cain's worthless offerings)

CONSIDER

If you are unused to devotional writings of the first millennium, this initial plunge may seem bewildering. In contrast to today's emphasis on reassurance, this prayer is raw and challenging. Do you judge it too alien, or inapplicable to your situation? Consider letting it judge you, in a sense, and to allow yourself to be brought into line with an earlier attitude toward the urgency of sin. For the ancient Christians, repentance was a gift which must be sought and prayed for; it doesn't come naturally, because we are so blind to our true selves. Yet that self-knowledge is the only way to liberation and joy. Are you willing to ask God to help you acquire true repentance?

5. Woe to thee, miserable soul! How like thou art to the first Eve! For thou hast looked in wickedness and wast grievously wounded; thou hast touched the tree and rashly tasted the deceptive food.

Have mercy on me, O God, have mercy on me.

6. Instead of the visible Eve, I have the Eve of the mind: the passionate thought in my flesh, showing me what seems sweet; yet whenever I taste from it, I find it bitter.

Have mercy on me, O God, have mercy on me.

7. Adam was justly banished from Eden because he disobeyed one commandment of Thine, O Savior. What then shall I suffer, for I am always rejecting Thy words of life?

Have mercy on me, O God, have mercy on me.

8. By my own free choice I have incurred the guilt of Cain's murder. I have killed my conscience, bringing the flesh to life and making war upon the soul by my wicked actions.

Have mercy on me, O God, have mercy on me.

9. O Jesus, I have not been like Abel in his righteousness. Never have I offered Thee acceptable gifts or godly actions, a pure sacrifice or a life unblemished.

Have mercy on me, O God, have mercy on me.

10. Like Cain, O miserable soul, we too have offered, to the Creator of all, defiled actions and a polluted sacrifice and a worthless life; and so we also are condemned.

Have mercy on me, O God, have mercy on me.

CHAPTER 2

EXPLORE

11. **"As the potter molds the clay."** (Genesis 2:7) "[T]he LORD God formed man of dust from the ground, and breathed into his nostrils the breath of life; and man became a living being." Note that the life within us is God's own life. The life of all Creation is in Him.

"I went down to the potter's house. . . . And the vessel he was making of clay was spoiled in the potter's hand, and he reworked it into another vessel, as it seemed good to the potter to do" (Jeremiah 18:3-4).

"Has the potter no right over the clay?" (Romans 9:21).

12. **"Sins I have committed."** Note that sins are not primarily seen as bad deeds that merit punishment. They are **"wounds"** which are **"inflicted inwardly"** by his **"murderous thoughts."** Though these are his own thoughts, he is the victim of them.

"Like thieves." (Luke 10:30) The man who "fell among robbers, who stripped him and beat him." Christ, like the good Samaritan, will have compassion on us and heal us.

"The thief comes only to steal and kill and destroy" (John 10:10).

13. **"Thou art full of loving-kindness."** Christ came to die for us "while we were yet sinners" (Romans 5:8). Our woundedness moves God to **"compassion"** and even his chastisement is **"in mercy."**

14. **"An outcast before your gate."** (Luke 16:20, Lazarus the poor man)

"In my old age." (Psalm 71:9) "Do not cast me off in the time of old age; forsake me not when my strength is spent."

CHAPTER 2

11. As the potter molds the clay, Thou hast fashioned me, giving me flesh and bones, breath, and life. But accept me in repentance, O my Maker and Deliverer and Judge.

   Have mercy on me, O God, have mercy on me.

12. I confess to Thee, O Savior, the sins I have committed, the wounds of my soul and body, which murderous thoughts, like thieves, have inflicted inwardly upon me.

   Have mercy on me, O God, have mercy on me.

13. Though I have sinned, O Savior, yet I know that Thou art full of loving-kindness. Thou dost chastise with mercy and art fervent in compassion. Thou dost see me weeping and dost run to meet me, like the Father calling back the prodigal son.

   Have mercy on me, O God, have mercy on me.

14. I lie as an outcast before Thy gate, O Savior. In my old age cast me not down empty into hell; but, before the end comes, in Thy love grant me remission of sins.

   Have mercy on me, O God, have mercy on me.

15. St. Andrew returns to the analogy of the man who fell among thieves, mentioned in verse 12 (Luke 10:30). Note again the concept that it is his thoughts which have wounded his body.

16. "The priest saw me first." (Luke 10:31–33)

"Despised my nakedness." In Canticle Two, St. Andrew will return to this theme of nakedness; the first effect of the Fall was that Adam and Eve realized they were naked.

17. "O Lamb of God." (John 1:29) "Behold, the Lamb of God, who takes away the sin of the world!"

"Take from me the heavy yoke of sin" recalls Christ's invitation, "Come to me, all who labor and are heavy laden, and I will give you rest. . . . For my yoke is easy, and my burden is light" (Matthew 11:28–30). Sins and sinful thoughts are a heavy yoke to bear.

"In Thy compassion grant me remission of sins." St. Andrew repeats this appeal three times, here and in the following verses. There is not any doubt that God will grant remission of sins; He comes running toward us like the father of the prodigal son. But we have to practice asking for forgiveness. The humility to admit the truth about ourselves, and to see that God loves us all the same, is the truth that sets us free.

15. I am the man who fell among thieves, even my own thoughts; they have covered all my body with wounds, and I lie beaten and bruised. But come to me, O Christ my Savior, and heal me.

   Have mercy on me, O God, have mercy on me.

16. The priest saw me first, but passed by on the other side; the Levite looked on me in my distress, but despised my nakedness. O Jesus, sprung from Mary, do Thou come to me and take pity on me.

   Have mercy on me, O God, have mercy on me.

17. O Lamb of God, that takest away the sins of all, take from me the heavy yoke of sin, and in Thy compassion grant me remission of sins.

   Have mercy on me, O God, have mercy on me.

18. It is time for repentance: to Thee I come, my Creator. Take from me the heavy yoke of sin, and in Thy compassion grant me remission of sins.

   Have mercy on me, O God, have mercy on me.

19. Reject me not, O Savior: cast me not away from Thy presence. Take from me the heavy yoke of sin and in Thy compassion grant me remission of sins.

   Have mercy on me, O God, have mercy on me.

20. **"All mine offenses, voluntary and involuntary, manifest and hidden, known and unknown . . ."** How can we be culpable for sins that were involuntary or unknown? Culpability is not the point. Even things we do in ignorance may injure God's creation or hurt other people. For example, along the beaches where I grew up, beautiful sea oats line the dunes. Visitors might pick them because they look attractive, not realizing that they play a vital role in preventing erosion. We can do harm without realizing it, and we can be just as sorry for those mistakes as for anything we do deliberately.

CONSIDER

What thoughts trouble you and provoke you to sin? These may not be simply outright goads to sin, but thoughts that fill you with fear or anger. The devil's prime weapon is confusion, and a darkened mind will misperceive the world and react destructively. Which lines of thought habitually lead you away from God into negative or defensive reactions? Do you see ways that these thoughts wound you? With practice, you can become aware of them and resist them before they lure you astray.

Have you ever said something casually, and later learned that it must have hurt one of your hearers very deeply? Of course, there may have been many such occasions where you never learned of the pain you'd caused. Ponder ways that you may have hurt other people, or God's world, unintentionally or without being aware of it. Can you feel sorry for these involuntary sin?

COMMENTARY
CHAPTER 3

EXPLORE

21. **"Ruled by the passions."** In early Christian writings, "the passions" refer to the impulses of our souls and bodies which were intended by God to serve us—for example, hunger, which is designed to prompt us to take in food for bodily strength. But since the Fall of Adam and Eve, the passions are distorted and rule over instead of serving us. The goal is to gain resistance to these impulses and turn them again to their right uses. For example, the passion of anger can be redirected into courage for fighting sin and doing God's will.

20. All mine offenses, voluntary and involuntary, manifest and hidden, known and unknown, do Thou forgive, O Savior, for Thou art God; be merciful and save me.

Have mercy on me, O God, have mercy on me.

CHAPTER 3

21. From my youth, O Savior, I have rejected Thy commandments. Ruled by the passions, I have passed my whole life in heedlessness and sloth. Therefore I cry to Thee, O Savior, even now at the end: Save me.

Have mercy on me, O God, have mercy on me.

22. "As the prodigal." (Luke 15:11–24, the parable of the prodigal son)

"O compassionate Father, come quickly out to meet me." Confident expectation of mercy draws repentance out of hiding, by taking away our fear.

23. "Grant me tears of compunction." God wants us to repent of our sins, not suffer because of them. It is the evil one, not our Father, who delights in human suffering. (1 Timothy 2:4) God "desires all men to be saved and to come to the knowledge of the truth."

"As I live, says the Lord GOD, I have no pleasure in the death of the wicked, but that the wicked turn from his way and live; turn back, turn back from your evil ways; for why will you die, O house of Israel?" (Ezekiel 33:11).

Note that in both these Scriptures salvation is bound to accepting the truth and turning away from evil. "For why will you die?" Death is the natural result of sin, not a contrived punishment. Communion with God is life. His overflowing forgiveness calls us into His life, but we must turn toward it and accept it, and "come to knowledge of the truth."

24. "Enter not into judgment with me." (Psalm 143:2) "Enter not into judgment with thy servant; for no man living is righteous before thee."

Note that sins are not solely the things we have done, but the things we "should have done."

"Overlook my sins." (John 5:24) "Truly, truly, I say to you, he who hears my word and believes him who sent me, has eternal life; he does not come into judgment, but has passed from death to life."

25. The first canticle closes with petitions that ask saints to pray for us. "Holy Mother Mary" is not the Virgin Mary, but St. Mary of Egypt.

This petition asks St. Mary to give us "the light of grace," but it should not be understood as saying that St. Mary is in charge of managing God's grace. It is a shorthand way of asking her to pray that we be given God's grace. Grace, by the way, is not a created thing that God sends us, but it is the presence of God Himself, "everywhere present and filling all things," as the ancient prayer to the Holy Spirit says.

22. As the prodigal, O Savior, I have wasted the substance of my soul in riotous living, and I am barren of the virtues of holiness. In my hunger I cry: O compassionate Father, come quickly out to meet me and take pity on me.

Have mercy on me, O God, have mercy on me.

23. I fall down, Jesus, at Thy feet: I have sinned against Thee, be merciful to me. Take from me the heavy yoke of sin, and in Thy compassion grant me tears of compunction.

Have mercy on me, O God, have mercy on me.

24. Enter not into judgment with me, bringing before me the things I should have done, examining my words and correcting my impulses. But in Thy mercy overlook my sins and save me, O Lord Almighty.

Have mercy on me, O God, have mercy on me.

25. Give me the light of grace, from God's providence on high, that I may flee from the darkness of the passions and sing fervently the joyful story of thy life, O Mary.

Holy Mother Mary, pray to God for us.

26. Bowing before the divine laws of Christ, thou hast drawn near to Him, forsaking the unbridled longings of sensual pleasure; and in fear of God thou hast gained all the virtues as if they were one.

27. This petition to St. Andrew was obviously added at a later date. It is fitting that a great author be remembered before God as we come to the end of a section of his work.

29. The last prayer in a sequence is often addressed to the Virgin Mary. She is called the "Theotokos," meaning "She who gave birth to God." Such a prayer is called a *theotokion*.

CONSIDER

Our tendency is to conceal and minimize our sins, thinking that God's compassion means that He will "go easy on us" and understand that "we're only human." This section of the Canon invites us to a different view: that all our sins are very serious (even those we don't know about), and yet God is abundant in mercy. He already knows all about our sins, and is ready to rush toward us in compassion. All that is necessary is for us to admit we *need* His compassion. Repentance is truth telling, and "the truth will make you free" (John 8:32). What hidden sins can you begin to admit, and allow God to take away?

How do you feel about the companionship of St. Mary of Egypt, St. Andrew, and the Theotokos? Is their presence alongside us in prayer helpful, or intimidating, or frankly not believable?

COMMENTARY
CHAPTER 4

EXPLORE

31. The first troparion, or *irmos*, of Canticle Two recalls the second Biblical Canticle, another Song of Moses:

"Give ear, O heavens, and I will speak; and let the earth hear the words of my mouth" (Deuteronomy 32:1–43).

In this hymn Moses recounts God's deeds of mercy toward Israel, despite their disobedience. This *irmos* focuses especially on the Incarnation, **"Christ, who took flesh from a Virgin."** When Christ took on human form He showed that the humble body of a human being could contain the presence of God. The good news of salvation begins in the manger.

Holy Father Andrew, pray to God for us.

27. Through thine intercessions, Andrew, deliver us from shameful passions and, we pray thee, make us now partakers of Christ's kingdom; for with faith and love we sing thy praises.

*Glory to the Father, and to the Son,
and to the Holy Spirit.*

28. Trinity beyond all being, worshiped in Unity, take from me the heavy yoke of sin, and in Thy compassion grant me tears of compunction.

Both now and ever and unto ages of ages. Amen.

29. O Theotokos, the hope and protection of those who sing thy praises, take from me the heavy yoke of sin and, pure Lady, accept me in repentance.

30. He is for me unto salvation Helper and Protector. He is my God and I glorify Him, God of my fathers is He and I exalt Him, for He is greatly glorified.

CHAPTER 4

CANTICLE TWO

31. Attend, O heaven, and I shall speak and sing in praise of Christ, who took flesh from a Virgin and came to dwell among us.

Have mercy on me, O God, have mercy on me.

32. Actually, it begins before that; nine months before, at the Annunciation. You will notice that almost all the praises directed to the Virgin Mary refer to her pregnancy or birth-giving. While we might praise another saint for eloquence in preaching or courage in the face of martyrdom, we praise the Virgin for offering the flesh and blood from which Christ took earthly form.

33. **"Look upon me . . . with Thy merciful eye."** (Proverbs 15:3) "The eyes of the LORD are in every place, keeping watch on the evil and the good."

"The eyes of the LORD are toward the righteous, and his ears toward their cry" (Psalm 34:15).

34. **"More than all men have I sinned."** (1 Timothy 1:15) "I am the foremost of sinners."

(Ephesians 3:8) "I am the very least of all the saints."

(Philippians 2:3) "In humility count others better than yourselves."

(Mark 9:35) ". . . be last of all and servant of all."

"I alone have sinned against Thee." (Psalm 51:4) "Against thee, thee only, have I sinned."

This assertion of St. Andrew, that he has sinned more than any other person, and ones later on where he states that he has committed every possible sin, are startling to contemporary readers. We feel that we could not agree to say such a thing, not out of pride but because it just isn't true. We see people in the newspapers every day who commit sins that we don't, and who are much worse than we are.

Yet somehow St. Paul could say this of himself, and he urged his readers to cultivate this way of thinking. He told them to have the same mind that is theirs in Christ, who emptied himself completely (Philippians 2:7). We are called to develop this habitual humility and frame of mind.

Two things make this possible. First is the shock of comprehending the holiness of God, and seeing how far short we fall in comparison. "Woe is me! . . . for I am a man of unclean lips!" (Isaiah 6:5). "Depart from me, for I am a sinful man, O Lord" (Luke 5:8). You can only make this statement about yourself; you don't have inside knowledge of anyone else, and you don't know what their limitations and struggles are. You only know the bitter darkness within yourself.

Second, the temptation to consider any other person worse than yourself lays an axe to the root of your soul. It is never warranted

32. Attend, O heaven, and I shall speak; give ear, O earth, to the voice of one who repents before God and sings His praise.

Have mercy on me, O God, have mercy on me.

33. Look upon me in compassion, O God, with Thy merciful eye, and accept my fervent confession.

Have mercy on me, O God, have mercy on me.

34. More than all men have I sinned; I alone have sinned against Thee. But, as God, take pity on Thy creation, O Savior.

Have mercy on me, O God, have mercy on me.

or wise to judge another. It is impossible to calculate your place on the spiritual ladder, and disastrous to try. Besides, God doesn't call on us to render an objective evaluation of anyone else's holiness; He reserves that to Himself. So as a mental act of discipline, stick by the assumption that you are the "foremost of sinners," and you will be in good company.

CONSIDER

The Desert Father Abba Macarius was met on the road by the devil, who struck at him repeatedly with a scythe, to no avail. The devil finally exclaimed, "What is your power, Macarius, that makes me powerless against you? All that you do, I do, too. You fast, so do I; you keep vigil, and I do not sleep at all. In one thing only do you beat me." When Abba Macarius asked what that could be, the devil replied, "Your humility. Because of that I can do nothing against you."

Reflect on your solitary standing before the glorious throne of God. There's nobody else around to blame or point at disparagingly. Discover the truth of St. Andrew's words in your own life: **"More than all men have I sinned."**

COMMENTARY
CHAPTER 5

EXPLORE

35. **"Stretch out Thine hand."** (Matthew 14:31) Peter sinking in the waves. Sin is confusing and tumultuous, like a stormy sea, and not always a clear-cut decision to do something you know is bad. It can seem like an attack of thoughts and impulses that try to overwhelm us. "Jesus immediately reached out His hand and caught him."

36. **"I offer to Thee . . . the tears of the harlot."** The woman who appears in Luke 7:36–50, a harlot who washed Jesus' feet with her tears, was a beloved figure in the early church. She represents the power of deep repentance, which opens the soul to Christ's healing mercy. "Standing behind him, at his feet, weeping, she began to wet his feet with her tears, and wiped them with the hair of her head" (Luke 7:38).

37. **"Darkened the beauty of my soul . . . turned my whole mind entirely into dust."** In the Greek text of the New Testament and

CHAPTER 5

35. I am surrounded by the storm of sin, O compassionate Lord. But stretch out Thine hand to me, as once Thou hast to Peter.

    Have mercy on me, O God, have mercy on me.

36. I offer to Thee, O merciful Lord, the tears of the harlot. Take pity on me, O Savior, in Thy compassion.

    Have mercy on me, O God, have mercy on me.

37. With the lusts of passion I have darkened the beauty of my soul, and turned my whole mind entirely into dust.

    Have mercy on me, O God, have mercy on me.

in early Christian writings, "mind" had a different meaning from the one we use today. The Greek word is *nous* (pronounced "noose"), and it did not mean the rational intellect. It's not easy to define, but it means something more like the perceptive power of the soul. The nous was created to connect us with the interior presence of God, and to be a living link with our Creator.

But ever since the Fall of Adam the *nous* has been damaged and **"darkened."** Its ability to hear God's voice is weakened. It is restless and hungry, and looks to be filled by anything that catches its attention. The ascetic struggle is directed toward training and restraining the nous, and causing it to attend once more to the life-giving presence of God. St. Paul wrote, "Be transformed by the renewal of your *nous*" (Romans 12:2).

38. This verse and many following ones reiterate the theme of being stripped naked by sin and left in shame. In Genesis 2:25 we see that "the man and his wife were both naked, and were not ashamed." But after prematurely taking the fruit of the tree of the knowledge of good and evil, before they had grown strong enough to assimilate this knowledge, their minds were wrecked and confused. "Then the eyes of both were opened, and they knew they were naked; and they sewed fig leaves together and made themselves aprons" (Genesis 3:7).

Shame at nakedness has to do with being seen by another person. People aren't ashamed to be naked in the shower. It's exposure to the gaze of others that causes anguish. The first wound of unbearable Knowledge was the realization that the beloved companion was other, was strange and alien and not wholly trustworthy. The first reaction is to conceal the true self, to hide—even from God.

41. **"All the ruling passions have plowed."** (Psalm 129:3) "The plowers plowed upon my back; they made long their furrows."

43. **"Garments of skin."** (Genesis 3:21)

CONSIDER

Have you had a dream about being naked in a public place? The sensation of shame is what makes it different from other bad dreams (like dreams involving physical danger). Shame is a curious emotion. It seems that we don't so much mind being the way we are—we just don't want other people to know about it.

38. I have torn the first garment that the Creator wove for me in the beginning, and now I lie naked.

Have mercy on me, O God, have mercy on me.

39. I have clothed myself in the torn coat that the serpent wove for me by his counsel, and I am ashamed.

Have mercy on me, O God, have mercy on me.

40. I looked upon the beauty of the tree and my mind was deceived; and now I lie naked and ashamed.

Have mercy on me, O God, have mercy on me.

41. All the ruling passions have plowed upon my back, making long furrows of wickedness.

Have mercy on me, O God, have mercy on me.

42. I have lost the beauty and glory with which I was first created; and now I lie naked and ashamed.

Have mercy on me, O God, have mercy on me.

43. Sin has stripped me of the robe that God once wove for me, and it has sewed for me garments of skin.

Have mercy on me, O God, have mercy on me.

44. I am clothed with the raiment of shame as with fig leaves, in condemnation of my self-willed passions.

Have mercy on me, O God, have mercy on me.

It is likely that you are not doing as good a job concealing your sins as you think. Best friends, family, and colleagues likely have a better grasp of your weaknesses than you think they do—perhaps even better than you do. Imagine lying on the ground **"naked and ashamed,"** no longer pretending ignorance of these sins. Join St. Andrew in asking God to rescue you, in His pity and compassion.

COMMENTARY
CHAPTER 6

EXPLORE

45. **"A garment that is . . . shamefully bloodstained."** This suggests the "garments of skin" with which the Lord clothed Adam and Eve (Genesis 3:21). Before the Fall, all earthly animals lived in harmony. But when the first couple were stricken by shame and compulsively tried to conceal their sin, this set in motion a cycle of bloodshed. Creatures now live by tooth and claw, at the cost of each other's lives. Adam and Eve are clothed in death—stinking, hairy, deteriorating, and bloody, a visible reminder of their estrangement from the source of life.

"[N]ot that we would be unclothed, but that we would be further clothed, so that what is mortal may be swallowed up by life" (2 Corinthians 5:4).

"Deliver me from bloodguiltiness, O God, thou God of my salvation" (Psalm 51:14).

46. **"Made in Thine image and likeness."** The enduring puzzle of humanity is that we retain elements of our resemblance to God our Creator, yet in every aspect we are also damaged and defiled. The church fathers found a helpful way to talk about this in Genesis 1:26: "Let us make man in our image, after our likeness." The **"image"** of God is impressed like a seal. It is indelible, and no matter how degraded a person is, or how far he wanders from God, he retains that image. But the **"likeness"** was corrupted in the Fall, and must be recovered. We do this by self-discipline, by avoiding sin and focusing our hearts on Him in prayer. We are in the process of learning to once again bear His likeness.

47. **"Hard pressed by the enemy."** (1 Samuel 13:6) The children of Israel hard pressed by the Philistines.

48. **"I wear a heavy yoke."** (Matthew 11:28–30)

CHAPTER 6

45. I am clad in a garment that is defiled and shamefully bloodstained by a life of passion and self-indulgence.

    Have mercy on me, O God, have mercy on me.

46. I have stained the garment of my flesh, O Savior, and defiled that which was made in Thine image and likeness.

    Have mercy on me, O God, have mercy on me.

47. I have fallen beneath the painful burden of the passions and the corruption of material things; and I am hard pressed by the enemy.

    Have mercy on me, O God, have mercy on me.

48. Instead of freedom from possessions, O Savior, I have pursued a life in love with material things; and now I wear a heavy yoke.

    Have mercy on me, O God, have mercy on me.

49. **"I have adorned the idol of my flesh with a many-colored coat of shameful thoughts."** (Genesis 37:3) Jacob "idolized" his favorite son, Joseph, and clothed him in an expensive tunic woven of various colors. This is a new variation on the theme of the clothing used to cover our nakedness.

"Little children, keep yourselves from idols." (1 John 5:21)

"Outward adornment . . . neglected that which is within." (1 Peter 3:3-4) "Let not yours be the outward adorning . . . but let it be the hidden person of the heart."

50. **"Tabernacle fashioned by God."** (1 Corinthians 6:19) ". . . your body is a temple of the Holy Spirit."

52. **"As once Thou hast sought the lost coin."** (Luke 15:8) The parable of the woman who sought her lost coin. As a coin bears an image of the king, we bear the image of our Creator.

CONSIDER

In what sense is your flesh an **"idol"** to you (verse 49)? St. Paul says that a man instinctively "nourishes and cherishes" his flesh (Ephesians 5:29). Even a person who hates himself does not "hate his own flesh," but will instinctively seek whatever makes his body content and comfortable. What is the difference between treating the body as an idol, and treating it as a temple? What is the difference between "adorning" and pampering the flesh by responding to its demands idolatrously, and honoring the body as the worthy and beautiful dwelling-place of the Holy Spirit?

49. I have adorned the idol of my flesh with a many-colored coat of shameful thoughts, and I am condemned.

Have mercy on me, O God, have mercy on me.

50. I have cared only for the outward adornment, and neglected that which is within—the tabernacle fashioned by God.

Have mercy on me, O God, have mercy on me.

51. With my lustful desires I have formed within myself the deformity of the passions and disfigured the beauty of my mind.

Have mercy on me, O God, have mercy on me.

52. I have discolored with the passions the first beauty of the image, O Savior. But seek me, as once Thou hast sought the lost coin, and find me.

Have mercy on me, O God, have mercy on me.

CHAPTER 7

EXPLORE

54. **"Like David I have fallen into lust."** (2 Samuel 11:2–4) David's adultery with Bathsheba. Sexual desire is not itself sinful, no more than hunger or thirst. But it is meant to be devoted to only one partner, the spouse. (Proverbs 5:15, "Drink water from your own cistern, flowing water from your own well.") Lust is desire self-indulgently directed toward others outside marriage, and may treat them as objects to be acquired, used, and discarded.

55. **"Like the publican I cry to Thee: Be merciful."** (Luke 18:13) "But the tax collector, standing far off, would not even lift up his eyes to heaven, but beat his breast, saying, 'God, be merciful to me a sinner!'" The figure of the publican, like the harlot, is an enduring example of humility and fruitful repentance. The ancient "Jesus Prayer," "Lord Jesus Christ, have mercy on me," derives in part from the publican's cry.

56. **"I have no tears."** Though we are well into the Canon, it is time to recognize how superficially we are treating all of this. We are going through the motions, unaffected by the words we mouth, perhaps motivated by intellectual curiosity, feeling no sincere repentance or compunction. We are numb. We must ask God for a miracle: that He will crack open our hardened hearts and stir us to feel repentance.

57. **"Lord, Lord."** (Matthew 7:21) "Not every one who says to me, 'Lord, Lord,' shall enter the kingdom of heaven, but he who does the will of my Father who is in heaven."

    "Shut not the door." (Matthew 25:10) While the Foolish Virgins delayed, "the bridegroom came, and those who were ready went in with him to the marriage feast; and the door was shut."

CHAPTER 7

53. Like the harlot I cry to Thee: I have sinned, I alone have sinned against Thee. Accept my tears also as sweet ointment, O Savior.

Have mercy on me, O God, have mercy on me.

54. Like David, I have fallen into lust and I am covered with filth; but wash me clean, O Savior, by my tears.

Have mercy on me, O God, have mercy on me.

55. Like the publican I cry to Thee: Be merciful, O Savior, be merciful to me. For no child of Adam has ever sinned against Thee as I have sinned.

Have mercy on me, O God, have mercy on me.

56. I have no tears, no repentance, no compunction; but as God do Thou Thyself, O Savior, bestow them on me.

Have mercy on me, O God, have mercy on me.

57. Lord, Lord, at the last day shut not Thy door against me; but open it to me, for I repent before Thee.

Have mercy on me, O God, have mercy on me.

58. **"Who desirest that all men shall be saved."** (1 Timothy 2:4)
60. **"Virgin alone worthy of all praise."** (Luke 1:42) St. Elizabeth's cry, "Blessed are you among women!"

"Intercede fervently for our salvation." (James 5:16) "Pray for one another, that you may be healed. The prayer of a righteous man has great power in its effects."

CONSIDER

We become so used to referring to "publicans and sinners" that we lose sight of how loathsome a character a tax-collector was in Jesus' time. These traitors collected money for the Roman government, and took advantage of general ignorance to collect as much as they could; they were legally entitled to keep the excess for themselves. (Imagine that America had lost World War II, and some turncoats skimmed money from the taxes they collected for Berlin.) These publicans were despised, yet they were not poor or oppressed; they were rich and oppressive.

Yet even they are welcome to God's mercy and forgiveness, and can receive it simply by asking for it. These "fatcats" will "go into the kingdom of God" (Matthew 21:31) before poor, oppressed religious people (like the Pharisees) who trust in their own righteousness.

It was to a centurion, a Roman military officer, that Jesus said, "[N]ot even in Israel have I found such faith. . . . many will come from east and west and sit at table with Abraham, Isaac, and Jacob in the kingdom of heaven, while the sons of the kingdom will be thrown into the outer darkness" (Matthew 8:10–12). Imagine Jesus giving this praise to a German general whose troops patrol New York.

This was a very offensive idea at the time, and it still is today. Picture the people whom you regard as too rich, powerful, and oppressive to enter the kingdom of God being seated at the banquet table. Is God more forgiving than you are?

58. O Lover of mankind, who desirest that all men shall be saved, in Thy goodness call me back and accept me in repentance.

Have mercy on me, O God, have mercy on me.

59. Give ear to the groaning of my soul, and accept the tears that fall from mine eyes: O Savior, save me.

Most Holy Theotokos, save us.

60. O Theotokos undefiled, Virgin alone worthy of all praise, intercede fervently for our salvation.

CHAPTER 8

EXPLORE

61. **"See now, see that I am God."** (Deuteronomy 32:39) The Second Canticle is unusual in that it is in two parts; the Theotokion in verse 60 ends the first section, and this new *irmos* starts the second. It likewise recalls a line in the second biblical canticle.

62. **"Give ear, my soul."** Whereas most of the Canon expresses our cry to God, here we are called to stop and listen. God seeks to save us: "O that today you would hearken to his voice!" (Psalm 95:7a).

63. **"To Cain and to Lamech."** (Genesis 4:8) Cain's murder of Abel.

    (Genesis 4:23) Lamech killed a "young man."

64. **"Thou hast not been like Seth, or followed Enos."** Early Christians considered Adam's son Seth (Genesis 4:25) and Seth's son Enosh (Genesis 4:26) to be righteous men like Abel.

    "Enoch, who was translated to heaven." Enoch was the son of Cain, and turned out much better than his father. Genesis 5:24 says "Enoch walked with God; and he was not, for God took him." This was understood to mean that Enoch was taken to heaven directly, without experiencing death, like Elijah in the fiery chariot. Hebrews 11:5 says, "By faith Enoch was taken up so that he should not see death; and he was not found, because God had taken him."

CHAPTER 8

61. See now, see that I am God, who rained down manna in the days of old, and made springs of water flow from the rock, for My people in the wilderness, by My right hand and by My power alone.

   Have mercy on me, O God, have mercy on me.

62. "See now, see that I am God": give ear, my soul, to the Lord as He cries to thee. Forsake thy former sin, and fear Him as thy judge and God.

   Have mercy on me, O God, have mercy on me.

63. To whom shall I liken thee, O soul of many sins? Alas! to Cain and to Lamech. For thou hast stoned thy body to death with thine evil deeds, and killed thy mind with thy disordered longings.

   Have mercy on me, O God, have mercy on me.

64. Call to mind, my soul, all who lived before the Law. Thou hast not been like Seth, or followed Enos or Enoch, who was translated to heaven, or Noah; but thou art found destitute, without a share in the life of the righteous.

   Have mercy on me, O God, have mercy on me.

65. **"Opened the windows . . . flooded, as the earth."** (Genesis 7:11–13) The Flood of Noah.

66. **"And he cried aloud lamenting."** Here is one of the rare instances where the version of the Old Testament used by early Christians differs from the one we're familiar with. As we learned in the Introduction, the first Christians (including St. Paul and the authors of the New Testament) used as their Old Testament not a Hebrew text, but the Greek Septuagint translation made about 250 BC.

Our modern English translations, based on later Hebrew texts, depict Lamech as possibly exulting at his victory over the young man who struck him. But in the Septuagint, the version St. Andrew would have used, Lamech is mourning: "I have slain a man to my sorrow, and a young man to my grief." (Genesis 4:23)

67. The **"young man"** slain is his own soul and mind, destroyed by the passions.

68. **"Skillfully hast thou planned to build a tower."** (Genesis 11:3–8) The Tower of Babel.

CONSIDER

Verses 66 and 67 introduce the startling idea that sin is suicide. The impulses of the passions, which seem like the cravings for life, actually further our alienation and confinement in death. Verse 41 spoke of the **"ruling passions."** Which passions rule you?

65. Thou alone, my soul, hast opened the windows of the wrath of thy God, and thou hast flooded, as the earth, all thy flesh and deeds and life; and thou hast remained outside the ark of salvation.

Have mercy on me, O God, have mercy on me.

66. "I have slain a man to my grief and wounding," said Lamech, "and a young man to my hurt"; and he cried aloud lamenting. Dost thou not tremble then, my soul, for thou hast defiled thy flesh and polluted thy mind?

Have mercy on me, O God, have mercy on me.

67. Ah, how I have emulated Lamech, the murderer of old, slaying my soul as if it were a man, and my mind as if it were a young man. With sensual longings I have killed my body, as Cain the murderer killed his brother.

Have mercy on me, O God, have mercy on me.

68. Skillfully hast thou planned to build a tower, O my soul, and to establish a stronghold for thy lusts; but the Creator confounded thy designs and dashed thy devices to the ground.

Have mercy on me, O God, have mercy on me.

COMMENTARY
CHAPTER 9

EXPLORE

69. **"The wounds, the open sores and injuries"** are dealt by both **"the enemy's arrows"** and **"my freely chosen passions."** The evil one, our enemy, provokes us to self-injury through our susceptibility to the passions.

70. **"Burnt up the men of Sodom."** (Genesis 19:24) A rain of fire falls on the city of Sodom.

   "The fire of Gehenna." In ancient times the "valley of the son of Hinnom" was the site of a *tophet* or fire stove, where toddlers and babies were burnt alive as sacrifices to Molech and Baal. By New Testament times it was being used as a garbage pit, and a fire was kept continually burning there to dispose of everything from kitchen refuse to the corpses of executed criminals. (Burning treats a body like garbage; it utterly obliterates it, depriving the family of a beloved face and form to wash, clothe, and bury with dignity. For this reason Christians have historically refused cremation.)

   The Greek word for the Valley of Hinnom is Gehenna. Jesus used this term when referring to the eternal burning anguish that will be experienced by those who speak in anger (Matthew 5:22), or whose "eye," "hand," or "foot" leads them into sin (Matthew 5:29-30, 18:9, Mark 9:43–48), and also by the wicked Pharisees (Matthew 23:15, 33).

71. **"In My judgment."** (Deuteronomy 10:18) "He executes justice for the fatherless and the widow."

   (Psalm 68:5) "Father of the fatherless and protector of widows is God in his holy habitation."

72. **"Holy Mother Mary"** here is not the Virgin Mary, but St. Mary of Egypt. The fierce warning of verse 69 is balanced by a reminder of God's mercy to St. Mary. **"In His loving-kindness He stretched out His hand to thee in help."**

CHAPTER 9

69. I am wounded and smitten: see the enemy's arrows which have pierced my soul and body. See the wounds, the open sores and the injuries, I cry to Thee; see the blows inflicted by my freely chosen passions.

Have mercy on me, O God, have mercy on me.

70. Roused to anger by their transgressions, the Lord once rained down fire from heaven and burnt up the men of Sodom. And thou, my soul, hast kindled the fire of Gehenna, and there to thy bitter sorrow thou shalt burn.

Have mercy on me, O God, have mercy on me.

71. Know and see that I am God, searching out men's hearts and punishing their thoughts, reproving their actions and burning up their sins; and in My judgment I protect the orphan and the humble and the poor.

Holy Mother Mary, pray to God for us.

72. Sunk in the abyss of wickedness, O Mary, thou hast lifted up thine hands to the merciful God. And, as to Peter, in His loving-kindness He stretched out His hand to thee in help, seeking in every way thy conversion.

74. Among the concluding verses of this Canticle is added a request that St. Andrew will also pray for us. **"Let us see the love of our God."** In a paradox, repentance enables us to see God's love. It is when we admit we deserve condemnation that we are able to receive His mercy.

75. A familiar pattern at the conclusion of a prayer is **"Glory to the Father . . ."** followed by a prayer addressed to the Trinity.

76. Then **"Both now . . ."** and a *theotokion*, a verse addressed to the Virgin Theotokos.

77. In conclusion, the *irmos* of verse 61 is repeated.

CONSIDER

The concept of hell has largely vanished from contemporary Western Christianity. Even when it was current, a biblical understanding was difficult to achieve, because English translations use single the word hell to cover two different Greek terms, "Hades" and "Gehenna." But these are two different conditions, and neither is a "place" in the geographic sense. When we stand in the unveiled presence of God, we will experience His radiance as either warmth and love, or searing misery.

In the in-between time before the resurrection of all earthly life, all the departed experience a foretaste of their ultimate destiny. The blessed are in Paradise, awaiting resurrection (Luke 23:43, "Today you will be with me in Paradise"; 2 Corinthians 12:3, St. Paul was "caught up into Paradise"). The lost, on the other hand, wait in Hades, like the rich man who neglected Lazarus (Luke 16:23). Neither true heaven nor Gehenna-hell can be experienced yet, since they require bodily existence. Those will commence when the souls of the departed receive their resurrection bodies.

We tend to shrug off threats of hell, assuming it could never happen to us. Yet Jesus said that anyone who called his brother a fool would be cast into Gehenna (Matthew 5:22). Have you been angry with anyone in the last week? Jesus said that anyone who failed to forgive would not be forgiven (Matthew 6:15). Is there anyone in your life whom you have not forgiven? Search your conscience, and discover how much farther you have to go to have "the mind [nous] of Christ" (1 Corinthians 2:16).

Holy Mother Mary, pray to God for us.

73. With all eagerness and love thou hast run to Christ, turning from thy former path of sin, finding thy food in the trackless wilderness, and fulfilling in purity the commandments of God.

Holy Father Andrew, pray to God for us.

74. Let us see, O my soul, let us see the love of our God and Master for mankind; and before the end comes, with tears let us fall down before Him, crying: At the prayers of Andrew, O Savior, have mercy upon us.

Glory to the Father, and to the Son,
and to the Holy Spirit.

75. O Trinity uncreated and without beginning, O undivided Unity: accept me in repentance and save me, a sinner. I am Thy creation, reject me not; but spare me and deliver me from the fire of condemnation.

Both now and ever and unto ages of ages. Amen.

76. Most pure Lady, Mother of God, the hope of those who run to thee and the haven of the storm-tossed: pray to the merciful God, thy Creator and thy Son, that He may grant His mercy even to me.

77. See now, see that I am God, who rained down manna in the days of old, and made springs of water flow from the rock, for My people in the wilderness, by My right hand and by My power alone.

CHAPTER 10

EXPLORE

78. The *irmos* of Canticle Three recalls the third biblical canticle, the Song of Hannah.

    "Upon the unshaken rock." (1 Samuel 2:2) "[T]here is no rock like our God."

79. **"Rained down fire."** (Genesis 19:24) The destruction of Sodom.

80. **"Flee like Lot."** (Genesis 19:22) Lot and his family escape from Sodom before its destruction. The angels told him to run to the hills, but Lot protested that he could not reach them in time. He asked permission instead to take refuge in a nearby town of Zoar, begging that it be spared devastation since it was so small. (Genesis 19:20) "Let me escape there—is it not a little one?"

    Sodom and Gomorrah are consistently held forth as examples of extreme sin being punished by utter destruction. Throughout the Old and New Testaments, these places are pointed to as examples of uninhabitable wastelands, and sinful persons and cities are warned that they will share the fate of Sodom.

    The type of sin which these cities practiced is not the sole condition for this punishment; it could be the result of any kind of sin. Ezekiel 16:50 points to greed, inhospitality, and "abominable behavior" as the provocation for God's act. "This was the guilt of your sister Sodom: she and her daughters had pride, surfeit of food, and prosperous ease, but did not aid the poor and needy. They were haughty, and did abominable things before me." But the usual understanding is that this destruction was due to sexual sin. (Jude 1:7) They "acted immorally and indulged in unnatural lust."

81. **"Flee from destruction by the fire of God."** (Deuteronomy 4:24) "For the LORD your God is a devouring fire, a jealous God."

    (Hebrews 12:29) "For our God is a consuming fire"

CHAPTER 10

CANTICLE THREE

78. Upon the unshaken rock of Thy commandments, O Christ, make firm Thy Church.

Have mercy on me, O God, have mercy on me.

79. The Lord, my soul, once rained down fire from heaven and consumed the land of Sodom.

Have mercy on me, O God, have mercy on me.

80. O my soul, flee like Lot to the mountain, and take refuge in Zoar before it is too late.

Have mercy on me, O God, have mercy on me.

81. Flee from the flames, my soul, flee from the burning heat of Sodom, flee from destruction by the fire of God.

Have mercy on me, O God, have mercy on me.

82. I confess to Thee, O Savior; I have sinned, I have sinned against Thee. But in Thy compassion absolve and forgive me.

Have mercy on me, O God, have mercy on me.

83.   **"I alone have sinned against Thee, I have sinned more than all men."** St. Andrew repeats this challenging theme.

84.   **"Thou art the Good Shepherd."** (John 10:11a) "I am the good shepherd."

"The lamb that has strayed." (Psalm 119:176a) "I have gone astray like a lost sheep."

(Jeremiah 50:6) "My people have been lost sheep."

(Luke 15:4) "What man of you, having a hundred sheep, if he has lost one of them, does not leave the ninety-nine in the wilderness, and go after the one which is lost, until he finds it?"

87.   **"Hail, Throne of the Lord!"** The Virgin Theotokos, by bearing Christ in her womb, represents the Burning Bush which bore God's fire; she is the mercy seat and ark of the covenant; she is the throne of God. Her womb contained the Creator of all, making her body "more spacious than the heavens," as an ancient hymn says.

CONSIDER

The Roman Empire established a monumental system of law that was effective in regulating the whole of the ancient world. We descendants of that history understand the word **"justified"** in that legal sense. But in the Hebraic and Greek biblical sense, justice was a condition of harmony between God and all Creation. It was a relationship. In this kind of "justice," the members of the community are in peaceful unity with each other.

This is why repentance matters. Raw legalism, pursuing external justice, could have no use for repentance. Repentance does not effect repayment, so it is irrelevant. But we are justified because Christ loves us, and because we come to Him in humility and love. "Righteousness" is "right relationship," and a right relationship with Christ will cause His followers to behave like He does—not cowering before a code of "objective morality," but bearing "good fruit" (Matthew 7:17-18) from a healed heart.

Ponder the difference between these two ways of understanding "justification," the "courtroom" meaning and the "relationship" meaning. Which is more demanding? Which is more thorough? Which is more enduring?

PARACLETE PRESS
PO Box 1568
Orleans, MA 02653

We hope you will enjoy this book and find it useful in enriching your life.

Book title: _____

Your comments: _____

How you learned about this book: _____

Reasons why you bought this book: *(check all that apply)*

☐ SUBJECT   ☐ AUTHOR   ☐ ATTRACTIVE COVER   ☐ ATTRACTIVE INSIDE

☐ RECOMMENDATION OF FRIEND   ☐ RECOMMENDATION OF REVIEWER   ☐ GIFT

If purchased: Bookseller _____ City _____ State _____

Please send me a Paraclete Press catalog, I am particularly interested in: *(check all that apply)*

1. ☐ Spirituality   4. ☐ Prayer/Worship   8. ☐ Religious Traditions (Which ones?)
2. ☐ Spiritual Practices (Which ones?) 5. ☐ Catholic Inspiration
                      6. ☐ Orthodoxy
3. ☐ Theology   7. ☐ Fiction   9. ☐ Other

Name (PRINT) _____ Phone _____

Street _____ City _____ State _____ Zip _____

E-mail _____

Please send a Paraclete Press catalog to my friend:

Name (PRINT) _____ Phone _____

Street _____ City _____ State _____ Zip _____

PARACLETE PRESS

PO Box 1568 • Orleans, MA 02653 • Tel: 1-800-451-5006 • Fax: 508-255-5705

Available at better booksellers. Visit us online at www.paracletepress.com.

83. I alone have sinned against Thee, I have sinned more than all men; reject me not, O Christ my Savior.

   Have mercy on me, O God, have mercy on me.

84. Thou art the Good Shepherd: seek me, the lamb that has strayed, and do not forget me.

   Have mercy on me, O God, have mercy on me.

85. Thou art my beloved Jesus, Thou art my Creator; in Thee shall I be justified, O Savior.

   God, the Holy Trinity, have mercy on us.
86. O God, Trinity in Unity, save us from error and temptation and distress.

   Most Holy Theotokos, save us.
87. Hail, Womb that held God! Hail, Throne of the Lord! Hail, Mother of our life!

COMMENTARY
CHAPTER 11

EXPLORE

88. As in Canticle Two, there are two sections to Canticle Three, and this is the second *irmos*. It also reflects the language of the third biblical canticle, the Song of Hannah, in its reference to **"the rock."**

89. **"Thou art the Fountain of life."** (Psalm 36:9) "For with thee is the fountain of life; in thy light do we see light."

(John 4:14) "Whoever drinks of the water that I shall give him will never thirst; the water that I shall give him will become in him a spring of water welling up to eternal life."

(John 7:37-38) "Jesus stood up and proclaimed, 'If any one thirst, let him come to me and drink. He who believes in me, as the Scripture has said, "Out of his heart shall flow rivers of living water".'"

90. **"Days of Noah."** (Genesis 6:5–13) God decides to destroy all earthly life.

(Matthew 24:37–39) "As were the days of Noah, so will be the coming of the Son of man."

92. **"Ham, who mocked his father."** (Genesis 9:20–23). After the successful grounding of the ark and the re-establishment of life on earth, Noah planted a vineyard, and with the harvest made wine and became drunk. His son Ham saw Noah passed out and lolling naked in his tent, and thinking it was a funny sight, told his brothers, Shem and Japheth. But those two responded differently; putting a garment across their shoulders, they walked into the tent backwards and covered their father.

CHAPTER 11

88. O Lord, upon the rock of Thy commandments make firm my wavering heart, for Thou alone art holy and Lord.

   Have mercy on me, O God, have mercy on me.

89. For me Thou art the Fountain of life and the Destroyer of death; and from my heart I cry to Thee before the end: I have sinned, be merciful to me and save me.

   Have mercy on me, O God, have mercy on me.

90. I have followed the example, O Savior, of those who lived in wantonness in the days of Noah; and like them I am condemned to drown in the flood.

   Have mercy on me, O God, have mercy on me.

91. I have sinned, O Lord, I have sinned against Thee; be merciful to me. For there is no sinner whom I have not surpassed in my offenses.

   Have mercy on me, O God, have mercy on me.

92. O my soul, thou hast followed Ham, who mocked his father. Thou hast not covered thy neighbor's shame, walking backwards with averted face.

   Have mercy on me, O God, have mercy on me.

93. **"The blessing of Shem."** (Genesis 9:24–27) When Noah awoke and realized what had happened, he placed blessings on Shem and Japheth and a curse on Ham.

94. **"Land of Haran."** (Genesis 11:31–12:1) Abraham's father, Terah, settled in Haran. But God called Abraham [then, Abram] to leave this land and go to one where he would receive a great blessing.

   "Flows with incorruption." (Exodus 3:8) "I have come down to deliver them out of the hand of the Egyptians, and to bring them up out of that land to a good and broad land, a land flowing with milk and honey."

95. **"Abraham . . . left the land of his fathers and became a wanderer."** (Hebrews 11:8) "By faith Abraham obeyed when he was called to go out to a place which he was to receive as an inheritance; and he went out, not knowing where he was to go."

96. **"Hospitality to the angels . . . inherited the reward."** (Genesis 18:1–15) One hot day, Abraham was sitting by his tent near the oak of Mamre and saw three strangers approaching. As is the custom in the life-threatening, arid environment of the desert, he earnestly urged them to accept his hospitality. They turned out to be angels, and told him and his wife Sarah that, although they were extremely old, they would have a son. Isaac would inherit the promises God had made so many decades before.

CONSIDER

The action of Shem and Japheth is being held up here as an example. Instead of ridiculing others' failings, we should conceal them. There are warnings in the Fathers that someone who reveals another's sin is equally guilty before God. Recall times that you have exposed the sins of others, either in ridicule or in false "concern," rather than holding the troubled person in your private prayers.

93. O wretched soul, thou hast not inherited the blessing of Shem, nor hast thou received, like Japheth, a spacious domain in the land of forgiveness.

Have mercy on me, O God, have mercy on me.

94. O my soul, depart from sin, from the land of Haran, and come to the land that Abraham inherited, which flows with incorruption and eternal life.

Have mercy on me, O God, have mercy on me.

95. Thou hast heard, my soul, how Abraham in days of old left the land of his fathers and became a wanderer: Follow him in his choice.

Have mercy on me, O God, have mercy on me.

96. At the oak of Mamre the Patriarch gave hospitality to the angels, and in his old age he inherited the reward of the promise.

Have mercy on me, O God, have mercy on me.

CHAPTER 12

97. **"Offered mystically as a new and unwonted sacrifice."** (Genesis 22:1–14) Abraham took his son, Isaac, to offer as a sacrifice, at God's command. At the last moment God halted the offering and showed Abraham a ram, caught in a nearby thicket, to sacrifice instead.

98. **"Ishmael was driven out."** (Genesis 21:9–14) About a dozen years before Isaac's birth, Abraham had had a son, Ishmael, by his bondservant, Hagar. Sarah did not want Ishmael to claim an inheritance along with her son, so she demanded that he and his mother be driven out. Abraham hesitated, but complied after God told him that he would protect Ishmael and make of him another great nation.

99. **"Hagar the Egyptian"**: The mother of Ishmael, above. In the New Testament, Hagar and Sarah are understood to symbolize the Old and New Covenants. (Galatians 4:24–26) "Now this is an allegory: these women are two covenants. One is from Mount Sinai, bearing children for slavery; she is Hagar. Now Hagar is Mount Sinai in Arabia; she corresponds to the present Jerusalem, for she is in slavery with her children. But the Jerusalem above is free, and she is our mother."

100. **"The ladder that was shown to Jacob."** (Genesis 28:12) Jacob dreamed of a ladder stretching from the earth to heaven, with angels ascending and descending upon it.

CHAPTER 12

97. Thou knowest, O my miserable soul, how Isaac was offered mystically as a new and unwonted sacrifice to the Lord: Follow him in his choice.

Have mercy on me, O God, have mercy on me.

98. Thou hast heard—O my soul, be watchful!—how Ishmael was driven out as the child of a bondwoman. Take heed, lest the same thing happen to thee because of thy lust.

Have mercy on me, O God, have mercy on me.

99. O my soul, thou hast become like Hagar the Egyptian: Thy free choice has been enslaved, and thou hast borne as thy child a new Ishmael, stubborn willfulness.

Have mercy on me, O God, have mercy on me.

100. Thou knowest, my soul, the ladder that was shown to Jacob, reaching up from earth to heaven. Why hast thou not provided a foundation for it through thy godly actions?

Have mercy on me, O God, have mercy on me.

101. **"The example of Melchizedek."** (Genesis 14:18) After winning a battle, Abraham was greeted by a mysterious "Melchizedek, king of Salem" who was also "priest of God most high." Melchizedek brought out bread and wine and prayed a blessing for Abraham, and Abraham gave him a tenth of all he had.

In Hebrew, "Melchizedek" means "King of Righteousness," and "King of Salem" means "King of Peace." The attributes of bread and wine, and the fact that Abraham paid him a tithe, and the fact that he appears without any genealogy, all led early Christians to consider Melchizedek a representative of Christ. (Hebrews 7:1–28)

102. **"Pillar of salt."** (Genesis 19:26) Lot's wife gazed back at Sodom and was transformed into a pillar of salt.

"Take refuge in Zoar." (Genesis 19:22)

103. **"Flee from Sodom and Gomorrah."** (Genesis 19:17)

CONSIDER

The story of Abraham's sacrifice of Isaac is told with exquisite tenderness. When God gives this devastating order he precedes it by, "Take your son, your only son, Isaac, whom you love." The eloquent third-century writer Origen points out that God's stress on Abraham's tender love for his son makes the request for sacrifice all the more devastating. It takes three days to reach the place of sacrifice—three more days and nights for the father to prepare food and drink for his son, to enjoy the child's playful company, to sleep with the little one in his arms. As they climb to the fateful spot the child asks, "Daddy, where is the lamb for the burnt offering?"

Do you remember Abraham's reply? "God will provide himself the lamb for a burnt offering, my son."

Hebrews 11:19 tells us that Abraham was able to do all this because he knew God had promised that Isaac would continue his line. He knew that, somehow, Isaac would live. Even if he was killed, God would be able to raise him back to life. So, as he departed with the child to climb the mountain, he told his servants to wait where they were because "I and the lad will . . . come again to you" (Genesis 22:5).

Origen points out that Jesus said we should "do what Abraham did" (John 8:39). Think through what it would be like to sacrifice to God whatever is most precious to you, in the firm expectation that God can restore it.

48

101. Follow the example of Melchizedek, the priest of God, the King set apart, who was an image of the life of Christ among men in the world.

Have mercy on me, O God, have mercy on me.

102. Do not look back, my soul, and so be turned into a pillar of salt. Fear the example of the people of Sodom, and take refuge in Zoar.

Have mercy on me, O God, have mercy on me.

103. Flee, my soul, like Lot, from the burning of sin; flee from Sodom and Gomorrah; flee from the flame of every brutish desire.

Have mercy on me, O God, have mercy on me.

104. Have mercy, O Lord, have mercy on me, I cry to Thee, when Thou comest with Thine angels to give to every man due return for his deeds.

Have mercy on me, O God, have mercy on me.

105. Reject not, O Master, the prayer of those who sing Thy praises, but in Thy loving-kindness be merciful and grant forgiveness to them that ask with faith.

CHAPTER 13

EXPLORE

106.   "**Tempests and billows.**" (Luke 8:23-24) Christ calms the stormy sea.

"**Do thou keep me safe.**" As Canticle Three comes to an end, as with previous canticles, we encounter a number of petitions to saints that they will pray for us. But this one might seem to go too far; can St. Mary of Egypt, who is after all a human just like us, "keep us safe"? No, the implication is not that she has super-powers, but that her will is so united with the will of God that her prayers will be effective. This union is the goal for all of us, and like her, it will come to us through the path of repentance.

108.   "**Best of guides.**" Likewise, this endearment addressed to St. Andrew would not be intended to mean that he is literally a better guide than any other saint or even the Holy Spirit. The loving words offered to saints in these troparia should be read as being affectionate and admiring, like love letters.

109.   "**Worship Thy power.**" (Luke 8:46) "Jesus said, 'Some one touched me; for I perceive that power has gone forth from me.'" The Greek word for "power" is dynamis, which we readily recognize as the root for "dynamite." This helps correct our view of "power" as merely the authorization to do something (a cop has the power to write a speeding ticket.) The power of the Trinity whom we worship is an active force.

CHAPTER 13

Holy Mother Mary, pray to God for us.

106. I am held fast, O Mother, by the tempest and billows of sin: But do thou keep me safe and lead me to the haven of divine repentance.

Holy Mother Mary, pray to God for us.

107. O holy Mary, offer thy prayer of supplication to the compassionate Theotokos, and through thine intercessions open unto me the door that leads to God.

Holy Father Andrew, pray to God for us.

108. Through thy prayers grant even to me forgiveness of trespasses, O Andrew, Bishop of Crete, best of guides, leading us to the mysteries of repentance.

Glory to the Father, and to the Son, and to the Holy Spirit.

109. O simple Unity praised in Trinity of Persons, uncreated Nature without beginning, save us who in faith worship Thy power.

Both now and ever and unto ages of ages. Amen.

110. **"While still remaining Virgin."** The ever-virginity of the Theotokos is not mentioned in the Bible, but it is a belief treasured from very early in the Church's history. In that era when there were arguments about everything, this belief apparently was never a matter of controversy. After Christ was born of her, it was appropriate for her to abstain from sexual contact, as the children of Israel abstained at the time that God appeared on Mt. Sinai (Exodus 19:15). A Scripture commonly understood to refer to her ever-virginity is Ezekiel 44:2, "This gate shall remain shut; it shall not be opened, and no one shall enter by it; for the LORD, the God of Israel, has entered by it."

112. This troparion is not written by St. Andrew, but contributed by St. Joseph the Studite, a hymnographer who became a monk at the monastery of Studios at Constantinople in the late eighth century.

"May we . . . behold with joy the splendor of Christ's Passion." This indicates that the Canon is used during Great Lent as preparation for Holy Week.

113. This troparion is written by St. Theodore the Studite, brother of St. Joseph and abbot of the monastery of Studios. Under his leadership this abandoned monastery was re-founded and grew from twelve monks to almost a thousand.

CONSIDER

The word *dynamis* (power) is matched by another Greek word, energeia, which means "energy." *Dynamis* is the dynamite stick lying in a box; energeia is the explosion. Variations on *dynamis* and *energeia* appear dozens of times in the New Testament, but English translations tend to sound more formal, and conceal from us the hair-raising nature of life in Christ. St. Paul's urgent need to proclaim the gospel rings out more clearly in the Greek: "For this I labor struggling, according to His energy energizing in me in dynamis" (Colossians 1:29, author's translation).

Consider Philippians 2:12-13, "Therefore . . . work out your own salvation with fear and trembling, for God is [energizing] in you, both to will and to [energize] for his good pleasure." How is God's will energizing in you for your salvation?

52

110. O Mother of God, without knowing man thou hast given birth within time to the Son, who was begotten outside time from the Father; and, strange wonder! thou givest suck while still remaining virgin.

111. O Lord, upon the rock of Thy commandments make firm my wavering heart, for Thou alone art holy and Lord.

112. Divinely shining lights, eyewitnesses of the Savior, illuminate us in the darkness of this life, that we may now walk honestly as in the day; with the torch of abstinence may we drive out the passions of the night, and behold with joy the splendor of Christ's Passion.

Glory to the Father, and to the Son, and to the Holy Spirit.

113. O company of the twelve apostles, chosen by God, offer now to Christ your supplication, that we may all complete the course of the fast, saying our prayers with compunction and practicing the virtues with an eager heart; and so may we attain the glorious resurrection of Christ our God, bringing to Him praise and glory.

Both now and ever and unto ages of ages. Amen.

114. The Son and Word of God whom nothing can contain, in ways past speech and understanding was born from thee, O Theotokos. With the apostles pray to Him, that He may bestow true peace upon the inhabited earth and grant to us before the end forgiveness of our sins, in His boundless love counting thy servants worthy of the heavenly kingdom.

COMMENTARY
CHAPTER 14

EXPLORE

115. The Fourth Biblical Canticle is found in Habbakuk 3:2–19, the final chapter of that Old Testament book. Habbakuk was a prophet of the late seventh century, a contemporary of Jeremiah, who foresaw the devastating invasion by Chaldean armies. In the first chapters of his book he argues with God about whether this is just. The concluding canticle is a statement of love and trust unsurpassed in its eloquence.

This translation of the Canticle of Habbakuk is taken from the Septuagint, the Greek translation of the Old Testament used by Christians at the time of Christ and for the first centuries of the Church. A comparison with the Hebrew version shows many differences.

"O Lord, I heard Thy report, and I was afraid;

O Lord, I considered Thy works, and I was amazed."

This is a good example of the usual pattern of Hebrew poetry: a statement is made, and then repeated in different words. The poetry is made by repeating the same idea, rather than in the rhyme or meter of the words.

116. **"Between two living creatures."** (Exodus 25:18) The mercy seat that is the throne of God in the tabernacle is flanked by two cherubim.

117. **"In Thine anger shalt Thou remember mercy."** An enduring statement of trust in God's forgiveness.

"The Holy One out of a mountain overshadowed." This was understood by early Christians to refer to the virgin conception of the Lord. (Luke 1:35) "The angel said to her, 'The Holy Spirit will come upon you, and the power of the Most High will overshadow you; therefore the child to be born will be called holy, the Son of God.'"

119. **"Before his face shall the Word proceed."** The Greek term here is *logos*, (John 1:1) "In the beginning was the Logos".

CHAPTER 14

THE CANTICLE OF HABBAKUK
(Habbakuk 3:2–19)

115. O Lord, I have heard Thy report, and I was afraid; O Lord, I considered Thy works, and I was amazed.

116. Between two living creatures shalt Thou be known; when the years draw nigh, Thou shalt be acknowledged; when the season cometh, Thou shalt be shown forth; when my soul is troubled, in Thine anger shalt Thou remember mercy.

117. God shall come out of Teman, and the Holy One out of a mountain overshadowed and densely wooded.

118. His virtue hath covered the heavens, and the earth was full of His praise. And His brightness shall be as the light; horns are in His hands, and He hath established a mighty love of His strength.

119. Before His face shall the Word proceed, and He shall go forth for instruction at His feet.

120. **"He stood, and the earth was shaken."** (Isaiah 13:13)
"Therefore I will make the heavens tremble, and the earth will be
shaken out of its place, at the wrath of the LORD of hosts in the
day of his fierce anger."

124. **"The abyss gave forth her voice."** (Psalm 29:3) "The voice of
the LORD is upon the waters; the God of glory thunders, the
LORD, upon many waters."

CONSIDER

God never changes. So how can He **"remember"** mercy in the
middle of being angry? We time-bound mortals can only imagine
His experiencing a change in His emotions. But God's anger is,
in a mystery, the same thing as His mercy. His character is pure,
harmonious holiness. Those who reject Him find that they still
cannot escape Him: His unbearable presence then feels to them
like raging fire. Those who turn to Him in love find His presence
to be all they have ever looked for; it is light and warmth and
peace. Jesus said "My yoke is easy," but an ox only finds a yoke
easy if he goes in the same direction as the bigger ox yoked beside
him.

If you fear God's anger over something, it is because you are
still clutching it close; you have not yet revealed it fully to His
already-all-seeing sight and asked Him for His already-surrounding-
you mercy. Offer to God the thing you most fear to reveal, and
pray like the publican: "God, be merciful to me, a sinner!"

COMMENTARY
CHAPTER 2

EXPLORE

125. **"Lifted up was the sun, and the moon stood still."** (Joshua
10:13) At the victory of the children of Israel over the Amorites,
"The sun stood still, and the moon stayed, until the nation took
vengeance on their enemies."

120. He stood, and the earth was shaken; He beheld, and the nations melted away. The mountains were violently burst asunder, the everlasting hills melted away at His everlasting going forth.

121. Because of troubles, I looked upon the tents of the Ethiopians; even the tabernacles of the land of Midian were dismayed.

122. Nay, with the rivers wast Thou wroth, O Lord? Nay, against the rivers wast Thine anger, or against the sea Thine attack? For Thou shalt mount upon Thy horses, and Thy chariots are salvation.

123. Bending Thy bow, Thou shalt bend it against sceptres; the Lord saith: The land of rivers shall be rent asunder.

124. They shall see Thee, and the people shall be in travail, while Thou scatterest the courses of the waters; the abyss gave forth her voice and raised her form on high.

CHAPTER 15

125. Lifted up was the sun, and the moon stood still in her course; at the light shall Thy missiles go forth, at the brilliance of the gleam of Thy weapons.

127.   **"Thou wentest forth for the salvation of Thy people."** This was understood by early Christians to refer to Christ's descent in human form. (Philippians 2:5–7) "Christ Jesus, who, though he was in the form of God, did not count equality with God a thing to be grasped, but emptied himself, taking the form of a servant."

128.   **"Thou didst cast death . . . Thou didst lay fetters."** Christ descended into Hades and took captive our captors, death and the evil one.

(Ephesians 4:8-9) "Therefore it is said, 'When he ascended on high he led a host of captives, and he gave gifts to men.' In saying, 'He ascended,' what does it mean but that he had also descended into the lower parts of the earth?"

(Colossians 2:15) "He disarmed the principalities and powers and made a public example of them, triumphing over them in him."

131.   **"Trembling went into my bones."** (Psalm 22:14) "I am poured out like water, and all my bones are out of joint; my heart is like wax, it is melted within my breast." This is the psalm that begins, "My God, my God, why hast thou forsaken me?" which Jesus quotes from the cross (Matthew 27:46).

135.   The final verse as it appears in translations from the Hebrew is familiar and beloved: "GOD, the Lord, is my strength; he makes my feet like hinds' feet, he makes me tread upon my high places" (Habakkuk 3:19).

CONSIDER

Habbakuk predicts dire things in verses 133 and 134; there will be famine, vines and fields will fail, and livestock will perish. These images sound to us like familiar poetic devices, but for people living close to the land, they would be understood literally, and spell likely death. Yet in spite of that he **"will be glad"** in God and be victorious with **"His song."**

Imagine losing everything you have and being faced with probable starvation, not just for yourself but also those you love. Can you nevertheless be glad in God, and sing His song? If not, and these things were going to happen just the same, what would you do? What is the alternative?

126. With threatening shalt Thou diminish the earth, and with anger shalt Thou trample down nations.

127. Thou wentest forth for the salvation of Thy people, to save Thine anointed ones art Thou come.

128. Thou didst cast death upon the heads of transgressors, Thou didst lay fetters upon their neck at the end.

129. Thou hast cut asunder with fury the heads of the mighty; they shall quake within themselves, they shall break open their bridles, like the poor man that eateth in secret.

130. And Thou hast mounted Thy horses in the sea, and they trouble the many waters.

131. I kept watch, and my belly was troubled at the voice of the prayers of my lips; and trembling went into my bones, and within me my strength was troubled.

132. I will rest in the day of mine affliction, that I may go up to the people of my sojourning.

133. For the fig tree shall not bear fruit, and there shall be no increase for the vines; the labor of the olive shall fail, and the plains shall bear no food.

134. The sheep have failed from their grazing, and there are no oxen at the cribs. But as for me, in the Lord will I be glad, I will rejoice in God my Savior.

135. The Lord is my God and my might, and He will instruct my feet unto perfection. He mounteth me on high, that I might be victor with His song.

CHAPTER 16

EXPLORE

136. This verse recalls the first verse of the Canticle of Habbakuk, and along with the following verses was written by St. Joseph of Studios.

137. **"Enlightened by God."** The presence of the Holy Spirit within illuminates both soul and body. (Ephesians 1:17-18) "That the God of our Lord Jesus Christ, the Father of glory, may give you a spirit of wisdom and of revelation in the knowledge of him, having the eyes of your hearts enlightened."

In the early church, baptism was commonly referred to as "illumination." We see this use in the book of Hebrews, where the hearers are reminded of the struggle they had to undergo "after you were enlightened" (Hebrews 10:32). Those who have been enlightened have also tasted the body and blood of Christ in the Eucharist, and if they reject so great a gift they will not return to repentance. (Hebrews 6:4) "For it is impossible to restore again to repentance those who have once been enlightened, who have tasted the heavenly gift, and have become partakers of the Holy Spirit."

139. **"The drought of polytheism."** Ancient polytheistic faiths retained a hold on the lands of the Middle East for long centuries.

CHAPTER 16

136. O Lord, I have heard the mystery of Thy dispensation: I have considered Thy works, and I have glorified Thy Godhead.

Apostles of Christ, pray to God for us.

137. Enlightened by God, the apostles of Christ lived in abstinence; and by their divine mediation they help us in this season of the fast.

Apostles of Christ, pray to God for us.

138. As an instrument of twelve strings, the divine choir of the disciples sang a hymn of salvation, confounding the music of evil.

Apostles of Christ, pray to God for us.

139. Driving away the drought of polytheism, O all-blessed apostles, with the rain of the Spirit ye have watered all the earth.

Most Holy Theotokos, save us.

140. I have passed my life in arrogance: make me humble and save me, all-pure Lady, for thou hast borne the Lord who has exalted our humiliated nature.

141. This verse—again a variation on Habbakuk 3:2—and those following were also written by St.Theodore of Studios.

144. **"Became a vineyard."** (Isaiah 5:1) "Let me sing for my beloved a love song concerning his vineyard: My beloved had a vineyard on a very fertile hill."

   "The wine of the Spirit." (Acts 2:13) the disciples on Pentecost morning, filled with the Holy Spirit, are speaking in other languages. Some are astounded at this miracle, but others take it as mere babbling. "Others mocking said, 'They are filled with new wine.'"

146. **"Hail, fiery Throne!"** All these salutations to the Virgin recall things in the Bible that bore the presence of God. (Daniel 7:9) "[T]hrones were placed and one that was ancient of days took his seat; his raiment was white as snow, and the hair of his head like pure wool; his throne was fiery flames, its wheels were burning fire."

   "Hail, candlestick that bears the light!" (Exodus 25:31-32) God commands Moses to construct a lampstand for the Tabernacle. "And you shall make a lampstand of pure gold. The base and the shaft of the lampstand shall be made of hammered work; its cups, its capitals, and its flowers shall be of one piece with it; and there shall be six branches going out of its sides. . . ."

   "Hail, Mountain of sanctification!" The "mountain over-shadowed" of the Song of Habbakuk (verse 117). (Psalm 78:54) "And he brought them to his holy land, to the mountain which his right hand had won.")

   "Ark of life." (Exodus 25:10) "They shall make an ark of acacia wood." This verse is likening the Virgin Mary to the ark of the covenant, rather than the ark of Noah.

   "Tabernacle." (Exodus 26:1) "Moreover you shall make the tabernacle with ten curtains of fine twined linen and blue and purple and scarlet stuff."

   "Holy of Holies." (Exodus 26:33-34) "[T]he veil shall separate for you the holy place from the most holy. You shall put the mercy seat upon the ark of the testimony in the most holy place."

141. I have heard the report of Thee, O Lord, and was afraid; I have considered Thy works and glorified Thy power, O Master.

Apostles of Christ, pray to God for us.

142. O honored choir of the apostles, in your intercessions to the Maker of all, ask that He have mercy on us who sing your praises.

Apostles of Christ, pray to God for us.

143. As Christ's husbandmen, O apostles, ye have tilled the whole world with the word of God, and ye bring Him fruit at all times.

Apostles of Christ, pray to God for us.

144. Ye became a vineyard, O apostles, for Christ the well-beloved, and ye have made all the world to drink from the wine of the Spirit.

Glory to the Father, and to the Son, and to the Holy Spirit.

145. Trinity one in essence, without beginning and supreme in power, Father, Son and Holy Spirit: O God, Light and Life, guard Thy flock.

Both now and ever and unto ages of ages. Amen.

146. Hail, fiery Throne! Hail, Candlestick that bears the Light! Hail, Mountain of sanctification, Ark of life, Tabernacle and Holy of Holies!

In verse 140 we turn to the Theotokos and pray, **"I have passed my life in arrogance: make me humble and save me."** Humility is indispensable to salvation. This is hard for us contemporary Christians to grasp, because our favorite stories show us heroes standing up boldly and, we might say, arrogantly, and cutting their opponents down to size. They may do this with a weapon, or they may do this with clever words, but in any case we find the example thrilling, and crave an opportunity to do the same.

But Christ gave us an alternative response: He enveloped evil with love. He forgave those who had just split the flesh of His hands and feet with iron nails. This is not our idea of heroism; if this were a contemporary movie script, He would have called down "twelve legions of angels" (Matthew 26:53) and provided us a noisy and satisfying spectacle of revenge.

The mistake we make is in thinking that our earthly opponents are our enemies. Instead, they are hostages of the enemy. Christ died for them, and for us, and for all sinners. We must imitate Him, and in humility show our enemies love, in the hope that they will accept God's mercy too. (Romans 12:19, 21) "Beloved, never avenge yourselves, but leave it to the wrath of God . . . Do not be overcome by evil, but overcome evil with good." Name to yourself some enemies whom you need to love. Make a decision to "never avenge yourself," and ask God to bring them to the same joyous salvation He has for you.

COMMENTARY
CHAPTER 17

EXPLORE

148. Here we return to the Canon as written by St. Andrew; this is the *irmos* of Canticle Four, once again echoing the opening of the canticle of Habbakuk (verse 115).

149. **"Thou hast power to pardon sins."** (Mark 2:10-11) "'But that you may know that the Son of man has authority on earth to forgive sins'—he said to the paralytic—'I say to you, rise, take up your pallet and go home.'"

150. **"The end draws near."** (Matthew 24:33) "So also when you see all these things, you know that he is near, at the very gates."

147. I have heard the report of Thee, O Lord, and was afraid; I have considered Thy works and glorified Thy power, O Master.

CHAPTER 17

148. The prophet heard of Thy coming, O Lord, and he was afraid: how Thou wast to be born of a Virgin and revealed to men, and he said: "I have heard the report of Thee and I was afraid." Glory to Thy power, O Lord.

Have mercy on me, O God, have mercy on me.

149. O righteous Judge, despise not Thy works; forsake not Thy creation. I have sinned as a man, I alone, more than any other man, O Thou who lovest mankind. But as Lord of all Thou hast the power to pardon sins.

Have mercy on me, O God, have mercy on me.

150. The end draws near, my soul, the end draws near; yet thou dost not care or make ready. The time grows short, rise up: the Judge is at the door. The days of our life pass swiftly, as a dream, as a flower. Why do we trouble ourselves in vain?

Have mercy on me, O God, have mercy on me.

(Psalm 39:4-5, "Let me know how fleeting my life is! Behold, thou hast made my days a few handbreadths, and my lifetime is as nothing in thy sight.")

"As a flower." (Psalm 103:15) "As for man, his days are like grass; he flourishes like a flower of the field; for the wind passes over it, and it is gone, and its place knows it no more."

(Isaiah 40:6, 8) "All flesh is grass, and all its beauty is like the flower of the field. . . . The grass withers, the flower fades; but the word of our God will stand for ever."

152. **"No sin has there been in life . . . that I have not committed."** Like St. Paul, St. Andrew considers himself the "foremost" of sinners (1 Timothy 1:15).

153. **"Who knowest my heart."** (John 2:25) Jesus "knew all men and needed no one to bear witness of man; for he himself knew what was in man."

Here St. Andrew reverses Proverbs 21:2, "Every way of a man is right in his own eyes, but the LORD weighs the heart." He knows that his ways are not right. Yet he trusts in the Lord, who sees the yearnings of his inner being, to forgive him. (Psalm 51:17b) "[A] broken and contrite heart, O God, thou wilt not despise."

154. **"The ladder which the great Patriarch Jacob saw."** (Genesis 28:12) Jacob dreamed he saw a ladder stretching from earth to heaven.

"Action and knowledge" mean right behavior combined with right understanding.

"Be thou made new." (Romans 12:2a) "Do not be conformed to this world, but be transformed by the renewal of your mind [*nous*]."

(Titus 3:5) "[H]e saved us . . . by the washing of regeneration and renewal in the Holy Spirit."

155. **"To win his two wives."** (Genesis 29:16–30). Jacob loved Rachel, the younger daughter of Laban, and offered to labor for seven years in order to win her hand. The seven years of hard work with Laban's livestock "seemed to him but a few days because of the love he had for her" (Genesis 29:20). However, on the morning after the wedding night, Jacob found, not Rachel, but her older sister Leah lying beside him (Genesis 29:25, "And in the morning, behold, it was Leah!"). Laban had made the switch so that the older daughter would be married first. He then gave Jacob Rachel as well, and Jacob labored an additional seven years.

151. Awake, my soul, consider the actions which thou hast done; set them before thine eyes, and let the drops of thy tears fall. With boldness tell Christ of thy deeds and thoughts, and so be justified.

Have mercy on me, O God, have mercy on me.

152. No sin has there been in life, no evil deed, no wickedness, that I have not committed, O Savior. I have sinned as no one ever before, in mind, word and intent, in disposition, thought and act.

Have mercy on me, O God, have mercy on me.

153. For this I am condemned in my misery, for this I am convicted by the verdict of my own conscience, which is more compelling than all else in the world. O my Judge and Redeemer, who knowest my heart, spare and deliver and save me Thy servant.

Have mercy on me, O God, have mercy on me.

154. The ladder which the great patriarch Jacob saw of old is an example, O my soul, of approach through action and of ascent in knowledge. If then thou dost wish to live rightly in action and knowledge and contemplation, be thou made new.

Have mercy on me, O God, have mercy on me.

155. In privation Jacob the patriarch endured the burning heat by day and the frost by night, making daily gains of sheep and cattle, shepherding, wrestling and serving, to win his two wives.

Have mercy on me, O God, have mercy on me.

156. **"Leah had many children."** (Genesis 29:31) "When the LORD saw that Leah was hated, he opened her womb; but Rachel was barren."

"Rachel . . . endured much toil." (Genesis 35:17-18) After years of barrenness, Rachel had a son, Joseph. Eventually she conceived again, but died giving birth to her second son, Benjamin. She knew great grief.

(Jeremiah 31:15) "A voice is heard in Ramah, lamentation and bitter weeping. Rachel is weeping for her children; she refuses to be comforted for her children, because they are not."

157. **"The mind that sees God."** (Genesis 32:30) After wrestling with the angel, "Jacob called the name of the place Peniel, saying, 'For I have seen God face to face, and yet my life is preserved.'"

"Gain great merchandise." (Genesis 30:43) Jacob managed Laban's and his own flocks expertly. He "grew exceedingly rich, and had large flocks, maidservants and menservants, and camels and asses."

(Luke 19:13) "Calling ten of his servants, he gave them ten pounds, and said to them, 'Trade with these till I come.'"

CONSIDER

"So shalt thou reach by contemplation the innermost darkness" (verse 157). This seems a strange goal for those who follow Christ, the Light. Yet in following Him we must gradually let go of all our preconceived notions about Him. Any positive statement we make—for example, "God is Light"—pops images into our heads that are based on what we have experienced on earth. But no sunlight or lamplight or starlight that we have ever seen can convey what God is truly like. Every statement we make about Him is, in the end, an analogy to fleeting, earthly things. So every statement we make about Him, in the end, fails. If we cling to them insistently, we will be clutching nothing but a shadow.

We must give up the comprehensible God, the one lit by match-sticks of feeble human understanding. The God who knows us is beyond anything we can imagine. As far as our minds go, He is robed in incomprehensible darkness.

(Psalm 18:9–11) "He bowed the heavens, and came down; thick darkness was under his feet. He rode on a cherub, and flew; he came swiftly upon the wings of the wind. He made darkness his covering around him, his canopy thick clouds dark with water."

156. By the two wives, understand action and knowledge in contemplation. Leah is action, for she had many children; and Rachel is knowledge, for she endured great toil. And without toil, O my soul, neither action nor contemplation will succeed.

Have mercy on me, O God, have mercy on me.

157. Be watchful, O my soul, be full of courage like Jacob the great patriarch, that thou mayest acquire action with knowledge, and be named Israel, "the mind that sees God"; so shalt thou reach by contemplation the innermost darkness, and gain great merchandise.

Have mercy on me, O God, have mercy on me.

158. The great patriarch had the twelve patriarchs as children, and so he mystically established for thee, my soul, a ladder of ascent through action, in his wisdom setting his children as steps, by which thou canst mount upward.

Have mercy on me, O God, have mercy on me.

(Isaiah 55:8-9, "For my thoughts are not your thoughts, neither are your ways my ways, says the LORD.")

Think about knowing and trusting a God who is so far beyond our comprehension. It is healthy to feel a bit of fear. (Psalm 111:10a, "The fear of the LORD is the beginning of wisdom.")

COMMENTARY
CHAPTER 18

EXPLORE

159. **"The birthright of thy first beauty."** (Genesis 25:29–34) Jacob and Esau were twin sons of Isaac. Esau was born first, and had the inheritance rights of an eldest son. But one day, when he came in hungry from hunting, he found Jacob cooking red lentil pottage. Esau begged for some, and Jacob made an audacious offer: a bowl of stewed lentils in return for the rights of a first-born. Esau agreed. (Genesis 25:34) "[H]e ate and drank, and rose and went his way. Thus Esau despised his birthright."

160. **"Edom" means "red."** (Genesis 25:30) "'Let me eat some of that red pottage, for I am famished!' (Therefore his name was called Edom.)" St. Andrew adds an interpretation of "red" as referring to Esau's lust.

161. **"Job justified on a dunghill."** (Job 2:8) Job was covered with "loathsome sores" and he "took a potsherd with which to scrape himself, and sat among the ashes." Despite the devastating losses of his wealth, health, and family, Job continued to honor God. He said to his wife, (Job 2:10) "Shall we receive good at the hand of God, and shall we not receive evil?"

CHAPTER 18

159. Thou hast rivaled Esau the hated, O my soul, and given the birthright of thy first beauty to the supplanter; thou hast lost thy father's blessing and in thy wretchedness been twice supplanted, in action and in knowledge. Therefore repent now.

   Have mercy on me, O God, have mercy on me.

160. Esau was called Edom because of his raging lust for women; burning always with unrestrained desires and stained with sensual pleasure, he was named Edom, which means the red heat of a soul that loves sin.

   Have mercy on me, O God, have mercy on me.

161. Thou hast heard, O my soul, of Job justified on a dunghill, but thou hast not imitated his fortitude. In all thine experiences and trials and temptations, thou hast not kept firmly to thy purpose but hast proved inconstant.

   Have mercy on me, O God, have mercy on me.

162. Once he sat upon a throne, but now he sits upon a dunghill, naked and covered with sores. Once he was blessed with many children and admired by all, but suddenly he is childless and homeless. Yet he counted the dunghill as a palace and his sores as pearls.

   Have mercy on me, O God, have mercy on me.

163.   **"Man of great wealth."** Job 1:1–22 recounts Job's former life. Though wealthy, he was just and devout.

164.   **"Snares and pits of the deceiver."** (Job 2:3–6) Satan makes a plan to destroy Job.

165.   Our wounds are like those of Job. Though he was unjustly attacked by **"the deceiver,"** and we are usually complicit in our own downfall, we can like him turn to God in helplessness and beg for healing. Christ the physician heals us, **"body and spirit . . . through repentance."** There is an echo of the good Samaritan. (Luke 10:33-34) "he had compassion, and went to him and bound up his wounds, pouring on oil and wine."

   "Wash, purify, and cleanse me." (Psalm 51:2) "[W]ash me thoroughly from my iniquity, and cleanse me from my sin!"

   "Whiter than snow." (Psalm 51:7) "Wash me, and I shall be whiter than snow." For dwellers in the arid Holy Land, snow and rain are uncommon enough to be signs of God's blessing. As this moisture softens the hard earth, new life comes forth.

166.   **"Thy body to refashion me."** (Luke 22:19) "This is my body which is given for you. Do this in remembrance of me."

   "Thy blood to wash me clean." (Luke 22:20) "This cup which is poured out for you is the new covenant in my blood."

   "Thou hast given up Thy spirit." (Luke 23:46) "Then Jesus, crying with a loud voice, said, 'Father, into thy hands I commit my spirit!'"

167.   **"Worked salvation in the midst of the earth."** (Psalm 74:12) "Yet God my king is from of old, working salvation in the midst of the earth."

   "Eden, closed till then." (Genesis 3:23-24) "[T]he LORD God sent [Adam] forth from the garden of Eden. . . . [A]t the east of the Garden of Eden he placed the cherubim, and a flaming sword which turned every way, to guard the way to the tree of life."

   "Things above and things below." (Philippians 2:10) "At the name of Jesus every knee should bow, in heaven and on earth and under the earth."

   (Revelation 5:13) "I heard every creature in heaven and on earth and under the earth and in the sea, and all therein, saying, 'To him who sits upon the throne and to the Lamb be blessing and honor and glory and might for ever and ever!'"

163. A man of great wealth and righteous, abounding in riches and cattle, clothed in royal dignity, in crown and purple robe, Job became suddenly a beggar, stripped of wealth, glory and kingship.

Have mercy on me, O God, have mercy on me.

164. If he who was righteous and blameless above all men did not escape the snares and pits of the deceiver, what wilt thou do, wretched and sin-loving soul, when some sudden misfortune befalls thee?

Have mercy on me, O God, have mercy on me.

165. I have defiled my body, I have stained my spirit, and I am all covered with wounds: but as physician, O Christ, heal both body and spirit for me through repentance. Wash, purify, and cleanse me, O my Savior, and make me whiter than snow.

Have mercy on me, O God, have mercy on me.

166. Thy body and Thy blood, O Word, Thou hast offered at Thy crucifixion for the sake of all: Thy body to refashion me, Thy blood to wash me clean; and Thou hast given up Thy spirit, O Christ, to bring me to Thy Father.

Have mercy on me, O God, have mercy on me.

167. O Creator, Thou hast worked salvation in the midst of the earth, that we might be saved. Thou wast crucified of Thine own will upon the tree; and Eden, closed till then, was opened. Things above and things below, the creation and all peoples have been saved and worship Thee.

Have mercy on me, O God, have mercy on me.

168.   **"The blood from Thy side."** (John 19:34) "But one of the soldiers pierced his side with a spear, and at once there came out blood and water."

"Drink Thy words of life." (John 4:14) "[W]hoever drinks of the water that I shall give him will never thirst; the water that I shall give him will become in him a spring of water welling up to eternal life."

(Acts 7:38) "[H]e received living oracles to give to us."

169.   **"Deprived of the bridal chamber, of the wedding and the supper."** (Matthew 25:1–13) The parable of the wise and foolish virgins. These virgins were supposed to greet the bridegroom when he came for the feast, but when he delayed all feel asleep. When he arrived at midnight, the foolish virgins awoke and found they did not have enough oil for their lamps. They went out to buy oil, and returned to find the door shut.

"Bound hand and foot, and cast out." (Matthew 22:2–14) Another parable about a wedding feast. The host of the celebration, the king, discovers an uninvited guest who has been revealed by his lack of proper attire. (Matthew 22:13) "Bind him hand and foot, and cast him into the outer darkness; there men will weep and gnash their teeth."

CONSIDER

Verse 167 says, **"The creation and all peoples have been saved."** Through Christ's victory, all God's Creation has been reclaimed as His, and has been freed from death and the evil one. But though we have been freed from these external chains, God will not violate our right to cling to internal shackles. (Galatians 5:1a) "For freedom Christ has set us free." It would be contrary to freedom for Him to force us to accept freedom. Everyone who comes into the marriage feast comes in of his own free will.

In Jesus' parable, the interloper at the king's feast is not appropriately dressed. No guest at the "marriage supper of the Lamb" (Revelation 19:9), can appear clad in resentment or unforgiveness or other garments "spotted by the flesh" (Jude 1:23). What unworthy garments do you cling to, which will show you unprepared for the Lamb's wedding feast?

168. May the blood from Thy side be to me a cleansing fount, and may the water that flows with it be a drink of forgiveness. May I be purified by both, O Word, anointed and refreshed, having as chrism and drink Thy words of life.

Have mercy on me, O God, have mercy on me.

169. I am deprived of the bridal chamber, of the wedding and the supper; for want of oil my lamp has gone out; while I slept the door was closed; the supper has been eaten; I am bound hand and foot, and cast out.

Have mercy on me, O God, have mercy on me.

CHAPTER 19

EXPLORE

170. **"Thy life-giving side."** (John 19:34) "But one of the soldiers pierced his side with a spear, and at once there came out blood and water."

"The two covenants, the Old and the New." The Old Covenant, (Exodus 24:8) "And Moses took the blood and threw it upon the people, and said, 'Behold the blood of the covenant which the LORD has made with you in accordance with all these words.'"

The New Covenant, (Matthew 26:28) "[T]his is my blood of the covenant, which is poured out for many for the forgiveness of sins."

171. **"Life is short, filled with trouble and evil."** (Genesis 47:9a) "Jacob said to Pharaoh, 'The days of the years of my sojourning are a hundred and thirty years; few and evil have been the days of the years of my life.'"

(Psalm 90:10) "The years of our life are threescore and ten, or even by reason of strength fourscore; yet their span is but toil and trouble; they are soon gone, and we fly away."

"Possession and food of the enemy." (1 Peter 5:8) "Your adversary the devil prowls around like a roaring lion, seeking some one to devour."

172. **"Speak boastfully . . . to no purpose."** (James 4:16) "[Y]ou boast in your arrogance. All such boasting is evil."

"Do not condemn me with the Pharisee." (Luke 18:9–14) The Pharisee boasted of his righteousness, but the publican humbly asked for mercy. The publican "went down to his house justified rather than the [Pharisee]."

CHAPTER 19

170. As a chalice, O my Savior, the Church has been granted Thy life-giving side, from which there flows down to us a two-fold stream of forgiveness and knowledge, representing the two Covenants, the Old and the New.

Have mercy on me, O God, have mercy on me.

171. The time of my life is short, filled with trouble and evil. But accept me in repentance and call me back to knowledge. Let me not become the possession and food of the enemy; but do Thou, O Savior, take pity on me.

Have mercy on me, O God, have mercy on me.

172. Now I speak boastfully, with boldness of heart; yet all to no purpose and in vain. O righteous Judge, who alone art compassionate, do not condemn me with the Pharisee; but grant me the abasement of the publican and number me with him.

Have mercy on me, O God, have mercy on me.

173. **"Violated the vessel of my flesh."** Sins of gluttony or misdirected sexuality violate the **"vessel of the flesh."** (1 Corinthians 6:15-16) "Shall I therefore take the members of Christ and make them members of a prostitute? Never! Do you not know that he who joins himself to a prostitute becomes one body with her?"

(2 Corinthians 4:6-7) "The light of the knowledge of the glory of God" shines in our hearts, and yet "we have this treasure in earthen vessels."

174. **"My own idol."** (Habakkuk 2:18) "The workman trusts in his own creation when he makes dumb idols!"

175. **"I have not hearkened to Thy voice."** (Exodus 23:22) "But if you hearken attentively to his voice and do all that I say, then I will be an enemy to your enemies and an adversary to your adversaries."

(Psalm 95:7b) "O that today you would hearken to his voice!"

177. **"An abyss of great iniquity."** Evil spirits are confined in the abyss. (Luke 8:31) the spirits infesting the Gerasene demoniac "begged [Jesus] not to command them to depart into the abyss."

173. I know, O compassionate Lord, that I have sinned and violated the vessel of my flesh. But accept me in repentance and call me back to knowledge. Let me not become the possession and food of the enemy; but do Thou, O Savior, take pity on me.

Have mercy on me, O God, have mercy on me.

174. I have become mine own idol, utterly defiling my soul with the passions, O compassionate Lord. But accept me in repentance and call me back to knowledge. Let me not become the possession and food of the enemy; but do Thou, O Savior, take pity on me.

Have mercy on me, O God, have mercy on me.

175. I have not hearkened to Thy voice, I have not heeded Thy Scripture, O Giver of the Law. But accept me in repentance and call me back to knowledge. Let me not become the possession and food of the enemy; but do Thou, O Savior, take pity on me.

Have mercy on me, O God, have mercy on me.

176. Thou hast lived a bodiless life in the body, O holy Mary, and thou hast received great grace from God. Protect us who honor thee with faith and, we entreat thee, deliver us by thy prayers from every trial.

Have mercy on me, O God, have mercy on me.

177. Thou wast brought down into an abyss of great iniquity, yet not held fast within it: but with better intent thou hast mounted through action to the height of virtue,

179. **"The thrice-holy hymn that is sung on high."** The **"thrice-holy"** hymn is "Holy, holy, holy is the LORD of hosts." This is the song sung by angels around the throne of God. The prophet Isaiah heard it in his vision in the temple (Isaiah 6:3), and St. John heard it in his vision on the island of Patmos (Revelation 4:8).

CONSIDER

Verse 180 contemplates the miracle of the Virgin Birth. **"He who is born makes new the laws of nature."** Some people object to the idea of miracles, saying that God has established certain laws in nature, and He would not break His own laws. They might find the idea of miracles disturbing or even frightening, since they suggest that this sober world could suddenly turn unpredictable.

But this legalistic view presumes that these "laws" of nature rule over God and restrict Him. No, instead these laws obey God and advance His will. God can do anything He likes, and whatever He likes will always have a dynamic, creation-restoring purpose.

The twentieth-century Serbian bishop, St. Nikolai Velimirovic, said that the world is like a train engine. We know that there is an engineer inside the cab. If the engineer puts his face out, waves a handkerchief, or tosses out a bag of mail, it certainly does not violate any "laws" of locomotion or damage one rivet of the engine. A child might be frightened at the noise and clamor of a train, but when the engineer looks out, he is reassured. "Oh, how dear it is to us when, from this mute universe which hurtles around us, someone resembling us appears and that someone is one who recognizes and loves us!"

"When God so wills, the natural order is overcome." Think about God's ability to overcome the natural order whenever He wills. Is this exciting news? Is it confusing, or frightening, or intimidating? If God is truly in control, there are no limits to what He might do, and that can make you feel uneasy when you stop to think about it. Yet the One who does these miracles is our Lord Jesus, the *"dear"* face that looks out from this hurtling creation.

past all expectation; and the angels, O Mary, were amazed at thee.

Holy Father Andrew, pray to God for us.

178. O Andrew, renowned among the fathers, glory of Crete, as thou standest before the Trinity supreme in Godhead, in thy prayers do not forget to ask that we may be delivered from torment, for we call upon thee with love as our advocate in heaven.

Glory to the Father, and to the Son, and to the Holy Spirit.

179. Undivided in Essence, unconfused in Persons, I confess Thee as God: Triune Deity, one in kingship and throne; and to Thee I raise the great thrice-holy hymn that is sung on high.

Both now and ever and unto ages of ages. Amen.

180. Thou givest birth and art a virgin, and in both thou remainest by nature inviolate. He who is born makes new the laws of nature, and thy womb brings forth without travail. When God so wills, the natural order is overcome; for He does whatever He wishes.

181. The prophet heard of Thy coming, O Lord, And he was afraid: how Thou wast to be born of a Virgin and revealed to men, and he said: "I have heard the report of Thee and I was afraid." Glory to Thy power, O Lord.

CHAPTER 20

EXPLORE

182. **"From the night."** The *irmos* of Canticle 5 recalls the fifth biblical canticle, the Song of Isaiah. (Isaiah 26:1–21) "My soul yearns for Thee in the night."

   "Give me light . . . and guide me in Thy commandments." (Psalm 119:105) "Thy word is a lamp to my feet and a light to my path."

183. **"The night of sin has covered me with darkness."** (Ephesians 5:8) "[O]nce you were darkness, but now you are light in the Lord; walk as children of light."

   (1 Thessalonians 5:5) "You are all sons of light and sons of the day; we are not of the night or of darkness."

184. **"Reuben's example."** (Genesis 35:22) Jacob's first son, Reuben, slept with his father's concubine Bilhah, who was the mother of two of his stepbrothers. Though he was the firstborn, this behavior won him a curse from his father: (Genesis 49:3-4) "Reuben, you are . . . pre-eminent in pride and pre-eminent in power. Unstable as water, you shall not have pre-eminence because you went up to your father's bed; then you defiled it—you went up to my couch!"

185. **"Brethren of Joseph."** (Genesis 37:19–28) Joseph had incurred the resentment of his eleven brothers by reporting dreams in which they bowed down to him in worship, and because he was their father's favorite. They made a plan to kill him, but changed their minds when a caravan of merchants bound for Egypt came into view, and instead they sold him as a slave. (Reuben, incidentally, did his best to save Joseph.)

186. **"As a figure of the Lord."** Joseph, honest and long-suffering, exhibited the character of the Lord Jesus.

CHAPTER 20

182. From the night I seek Thee early, O Lover of mankind: give me light, I pray Thee, and guide me in Thy commandments, and teach me, O Savior, to do Thy will.

Have mercy on me, O God, have mercy on me.

183. In night have I passed all my life: for the night of sin has covered me with darkness and thick mist. But make me, O Savior, a son of the day.

Have mercy on me, O God, have mercy on me.

184. In my misery I have followed Reuben's example, and have devised a wicked and unlawful plan against the Most High God, defiling my bed as he defiled his father's.

Have mercy on me, O God, have mercy on me.

185. I confess to Thee, O Christ my King: I have sinned, I have sinned like the brethren of Joseph, who once sold the fruit of purity and chastity.

Have mercy on me, O God, have mercy on me.

186. As a figure of the Lord, O my soul, the righteous and gentle Joseph was sold into bondage by his brethren;

187. **"Righteous and pure."** Joseph was also considered an example of chastity, because of the incident in Genesis 39:7–20. When he arrived in Egypt he was purchased by an official named Potiphar, and rose to high responsibility in his house. Potiphar's wife tried "day after day" (Genesis 39:10) to convince Joseph to "lie with her," but he always refused, citing his master's trust. At last she seized him by his clothing, but he ran away leaving his garment in her hand. She showed this to her husband, saying that Joseph had tried to rape her and had fled when she screamed. Potiphar had Joseph jailed. (By the way, the Septuagint describes Potiphar as a "eunuch," rather than an "officer," of Pharaoh, and this may explain his wife's desperation.)

188. **"Cast into a pit."** (Genesis 37:24) His brothers seized him and threw him in a dry pit, then drew him out and sold him when a caravan of traders came by. St. Andrew invites us to see this as foreshadowing Christ's burial and resurrection.

189. **"The bitter execution of Pharaoh's decree."** (Exodus 1:15–2:10) As the Hebrews began to multiply in Egypt they started to out-number their Egyptian rulers. Pharaoh ordered the Hebrew midwives to kill all newborn male babies (this brings to mind Herod's slaughter of the innocents after the birth of Christ), but the midwives "feared God" and refused to do so. Pharaoh then ordered his people to throw male Hebrew children into the Nile. When Moses was three months old his mother hid him in a basket at the edge of the Nile, where he was found by Pharaoh's daughter and raised in the Egyptian court. Happily, Moses' sister, Miriam, was watching when Moses was found, and offered to fetch a Hebrew wet-nurse. Pharaoh's daughter gave Moses back to his own mother, and paid her to care for him until he was weaned.

190. **"Like great Moses, be suckled on wisdom."** (Acts 7:22) "Moses was instructed in all the wisdom of the Egyptians, and he was mighty in his words and deeds."

191. **"Struck and killed the Egyptian mind."** (Exodus 2:11-12) Moses saw an Egyptian beating a Hebrew and killed him.

CONSIDER

In this section there are several images of enclosure and conceal-ment: Reuben **"devised a wicked . . . plan"** to sleep with his father's mistress, Joseph was thrown into a pit, Moses was hidden in a basket. Overarching these themes is the opening image of calling to God out of the night and darkness. What enclosures

but thou hast sold thyself entirely to thy sins.

Have mercy on me, O God, have mercy on me.

187. O miserable and wicked soul, imitate the righteous and pure mind of Joseph; and do not live in wantonness, sinfully indulging thy disordered desires.

Have mercy on me, O God, have mercy on me.

188. Once Joseph was cast into a pit, O Lord and Master, as a figure of Thy burial and resurrection. But what offering such as this shall I ever make to Thee?

Have mercy on me, O God, have mercy on me.

189. Thou hast heard, my soul, of the basket of Moses: how he was borne on the waves of the river as if in a shrine; and so he avoided the bitter execution of Pharaoh's decree.

Have mercy on me, O God, have mercy on me.

190. Thou hast heard, wretched soul, of the midwives who once killed in its infancy the manly action of self-control: like great Moses, then, be suckled on wisdom.

Have mercy on me, O God, have mercy on me.

191. O miserable soul, thou hast not struck and killed the Egyptian mind, as did Moses the great. Tell me, then, how wilt thou go to dwell through repentance in the wilderness empty of passions?

Have mercy on me, O God, have mercy on me.

surround you? Are some for your safety, such as Moses' basket? Are some confinements caused by others, like Joseph's pit, an act of malice that God ultimately used for good? Are some of your own devising—plans that further your own designs, but which lock you in the dark confusion of sin?

CHAPTER 21

EXPLORE

192. **"Moses went to dwell in the desert."** (Exodus 2:15) After slaying the Egyptian, Moses fled to the desert of Midian. Desert-dwelling is of course associated with the monastic life.

"Thou mayest attain the vision of God in the bush." (Exodus 3:1–6) While Moses was tending his flock in the wilderness, "the angel of the LORD appeared to him in a flame of fire out of the midst of a bush; and he looked, and lo, the bush was burning, yet it was not consumed." The Lord spoke to Moses from the bush and empowered him to lead the Hebrews to freedom.

This **"vision of God in the bush"** is, like the Transfiguration of Christ on Mt. Tabor (Matthew 17:1–8), the Christian destiny. By diligence in seeking God we are purified, then illumined, and then see His light; and to see His light is to be engulfed and filled by it. (1 John 3:2) "Beloved, we are God's children now; it does not yet appear what we shall be, but we know that when he appears we shall be like him, for we shall see him as he is." So wrote St. John, who had been a witness on Mt. Tabor.

193. **"The rod of Moses striking the sea."** (Exodus 14:10–22) The Hebrews, fleeing from Pharaoh's army, found themselves walled in by the Red Sea. In terror they berated Moses, saying "it would have been better for us to serve the Egyptians than to die in the wilderness." But the LORD said to Moses, "Lift up your rod, and stretch out your hand over the sea and divide it, that the people of Israel may go on dry ground through the sea. . . ." Then Moses stretched out his hand over the sea; and the LORD drove the sea back by a strong east wind all night, and made the sea dry land, and the waters were divided. And the people of Israel went into the midst of the sea on dry ground, the waters being a wall to them on their right hand and on their left.

194. St. Andrew sees the rod of Moses as a prefiguring of the cross.

CHAPTER 21

192. Moses the great went to dwell in the desert. Come, seek to follow his way of life, my soul, that in contemplation thou mayest attain the vision of God in the bush.

   Have mercy on me, O God, have mercy on me.

193. Picture to thyself, my soul, the rod of Moses striking the sea and making hard the deep by the sign of the holy cross. Through the Cross thou also canst do great things.

   Have mercy on me, O God, have mercy on me.

194. Aaron offered to God fire that was blameless and undefiled, but Hophni and Phinehas brought to Him, as thou hast done, my soul, strange fire and a polluted life.

   Have mercy on me, O God, have mercy on me.

(John 12:32) "[A]nd I, when I am lifted up from the earth, will draw all men to myself."

St. Andrew combines in this verse several Old Testament references to priests who mishandled holy things and offended God with immoral lives.

"Aaron offered to God fire that was blameless." Aaron was Moses' brother, the high priest. (Leviticus 9:22–24) "Aaron lifted up his hands toward the people and blessed them . . . And fire came forth from before the LORD and consumed the burnt offering and the fat upon the altar; and when all the people saw it, they shouted, and fell on their faces."

During the years in the wilderness, some Levites rose up against Moses in a power struggle. Aaron offered incense that was accepted by God, but the earth opened and swallowed the rebellious priests. (Numbers 16:1–40)

"Hophni and Phinehas." (1 Samuel 2:12–34) These were sons of Eli, the high priest who cared for the child Samuel, the young son of Hannah. Hophni and Phineas extorted shares from the offerings, and slept with women who served at the entrance of the tent of meeting. God swore to Eli that his sons' iniquity would never be forgiven. They were slain in a devastating battle in which the ark of the covenant was captured.

"Strange fire." (Leviticus 10:2) Aaron's sons Nadab and Abihu offered "unholy fire" to God. "Fire came forth from the presence of the LORD and devoured them. . . ."

195. **"Jannes and Jambres."** (Exodus 7:11) When Moses first appeared before Pharaoh and demonstrated miraculous powers, Pharaoh called on his magicians, who were able to replicate some of the feats. St. Paul compares fraudulent preachers to these magicians. (2 Timothy 3:8) "As Jannes and Jambres opposed Moses, so these men also oppose the truth. . . ."

196. **"Wash me clean."** (Psalm 51:2)
"White as snow." (Psalm 51:7)

CONSIDER

God's dealings with his erring priests seem harsh. Isn't He a God of forgiveness? But it is the same fire of God that Moses saw in the Burning Bush and that St. John saw transfiguring Christ on Mt. Tabor, which devoured Nadab and Abihu. People in earlier

195. In my soul and body, O Master, I have become like Jannes and Jambres the magicians of cruel Pharaoh; my will is heavy and my mind is drowned beneath the waters. But do Thou come to my aid.

   Have mercy on me, O God, have mercy on me.

196. Woe is me! I have defiled my mind with filth. I pray to Thee, O Master: Wash me clean in the waters of my tears and make the garment of my flesh white as snow.

   Have mercy on me, O God, have mercy on me.

197. When I examine my actions, O Savior, I see that I have gone beyond all men in sin; for I knew and understood what I did; I was not sinning in ignorance.

   Have mercy on me, O God, have mercy on me.

198. Spare, O spare the work of Thine hands, O Lord. I have sinned, forgive me: for Thou alone art pure by nature, and none save Thee is free from defilement.

   Have mercy on me, O God, have mercy on me.

generations had more familiarity with the characteristics of fire than we do. Until a hundred years ago, there was no experience of light that was not provided by fire, whether candlelight, lamplight, or campfire. All scriptural references to "light" assume the presence of fire.

Fire is brilliant, illuminating, and warming, but is also dangerous in its power. It must be treated with respect. Fire does not compromise or make allowances. In an encounter, any change that takes place will be on the part of the one approaching the fire—not the fire itself.

God is changeless by His very nature. If you approach Him, you are going to be the one doing the changing. (1 Corinthians 3:15) "If any man's work is burned up, he will suffer loss, though he himself will be saved, but only as through fire." What in you will be burned up when you meet the light of Christ?

COMMENTARY
CHAPTER 22

EXPLORE

199. **"Fashioned as I am."** (Philippians 2:5–7) "Christ Jesus, who, though he was in the form of God, did not count equality with God a thing to be grasped, but emptied himself, taking the form of a servant, being born in the likeness of men."

"Healing lepers." (Luke 17:12–19) The healing of ten lepers on the road.

"Strength to the paralyzed." (Luke 5:18–25) The healing of the paralytic who was let down through the roof by his friends.

"Woman who touched the hem." (Luke 8:43–48) The healing of the woman who had a flow of blood.) She did not dare ask Jesus directly for healing, but only touched the hem of his garment.

201. **"Woman who was bowed to the ground."** (Luke 13:11–13) This woman was bent over and could not straighten up, and had been that way for eighteen years. Jesus healed her, and was then challenged by the Pharisees for working on the Sabbath.

202. **"Woman of Samaria."** (John 4:5–30) While traveling through Samaria, Jesus sat down by a well to rest, and met a woman who came to draw water; she is known to the Church as St. Photini. (John 4:13–15) "Jesus said to her, 'Everyone who drinks of this water will thirst again, but whoever drinks of the water that I

CHAPTER 22

199. Thou who art God, O Savior, wast for my sake fashioned as I am. Thou hast performed miracles, healing lepers, giving strength to the paralyzed, stopping the issue of blood when the woman touched the hem of Thy garment.

Have mercy on me, O God, have mercy on me.

200. O wretched soul, do as the woman with an issue of blood: Run quickly, grasp the hem of the garment of Christ; so shalt thou be healed of thine afflictions and hear Him say, "Thy faith has saved thee."

Have mercy on me, O God, have mercy on me.

201. O my soul, do as the woman who was bowed to the ground. Fall at the feet of Jesus, that He may make thee straight again: and thou shalt walk upright upon the paths of the Lord.

Have mercy on me, O God, have mercy on me.

202. Thou art a deep well, O Master: Make springs gush forth for me from Thy pure veins, that like the woman of Samaria I may drink and thirst no more; for from Thee flow the streams of life.

Have mercy on me, O God, have mercy on me.

shall give him will never thirst; the water that I shall give him will become in him a spring of water welling up to eternal life.' The woman said to him, 'Sir, give me this water, that I may not thirst, nor come here to draw.'"

203. **"Siloam . . . wash clean the eyes of my soul."** (John 9:1–38) Jesus met a man born blind and healed him, telling him to go wash his eyes in the pool of Siloam. (John 9:7b) "So he went and washed and came back seeing."

    "The pre-eternal light." God was Himself light, before He created light to illumine the earth. (Genesis 1:3) "And God said, 'Let there be light'; and there was light." Earthly light beautifully evokes God's presence to our limited minds, but when we are fully healed we will behold the light that was before creation.

204. **"The wood of life."** St. Mary of Egypt was initially prevented from seeing the cross, when she first arrived at the church and found she could not cross the threshold.

205. **"Crossing the stream of the Jordan"** calls to mind the Hebrews' crossing of the Red Sea—a dramatic break that begins a new life in the purifying desert.

207. **"Holy, holy, holy art Thou."** We join in the hymn of the angels before the throne of God, as recorded in Isaiah 6:3 and Revelation 4:8.

208. **"From thee has God . . . taken human flesh."** Praise of the Virgin Theotokos always returns to her role in the Incarnation.

CONSIDER

In verses 199, 201, and 203 we are reminded of a number of healing miracles performed by our Lord, some of them very extraordinary. "Never since the world began has it been heard that any one opened the eyes of a man born blind" (John 9:32). Is there a physical or emotional healing that you yearn for? Have you, personally, experienced a healing, or heard of one among people you know?

Yet, extraordinary as these miracles are, St. Andrew is asking instead for a healing of soul. Every body that experiences a physical healing—even the body of one who has been raised from the dead, as Lazarus was—will die again and decay in the earth. But spiritual healing prepares us for eternity. How do you need the **"eyes of your soul"** to be washed clean and opened?

203. O Master and Lord, may my tears be unto me as Siloam: that I also may wash clean the eyes of my soul, and with my mind behold Thee, the pre-eternal Light.

Have mercy on me, O God, have mercy on me.

204. O blessed saint, with a love beyond compare thou hast longed to venerate the wood of life, and thy desire was granted. Make me also worthy to attain the glory on high.

Have mercy on me, O God, have mercy on me.

205. Crossing the stream of Jordan, thou hast found peace, escaping from the deadening pleasures of the flesh. Deliver us also from them, holy Mary, by thine intercessions.

Have mercy on me, O God, have mercy on me.

206. Best of shepherds, chosen above all others, O wise Andrew, with great love and fear I beseech thee: Through thine intercessions may I receive salvation and eternal life.

*Glory to the Father, and to the Son,
and to the Holy Spirit.*

207. We glorify Thee, O Trinity, the one God. Holy, holy, holy art Thou: Father, Son and Spirit, simple Essence and Unity, worshiped for ever.

Both now and ever and unto ages of ages. Amen.

208. O Virgin inviolate and Mother who hast not known man, from thee has God, the Creator of the ages, taken human flesh, uniting to Himself the nature of men.

CHAPTER 23

EXPLORE

210. Canticle Six begins with an *irmos* that recalls the sixth biblical canticle, the Song of Jonah. (Jonah 2:1-2) "Then Jonah prayed to the LORD his God from the belly of the fish, saying, 'I called to the LORD, out of my distress, and he answered me; out of the belly of Sheol I cried, and thou didst hear my voice.'"

211. **"Be merciful to me."** (Luke 18:13) "But the tax collector, standing far off, would not even lift up his eyes to heaven, but beat his breast, saying, 'God, be merciful to me a sinner!'"

212. **"Like Dathan and Abiram."** These were rebels who challenged Moses in the wilderness; the earth opened and swallowed their tents and all that belonged to them (Numbers 16:1–35).

   (Psalm 106:16-17) "When men in the camp were jealous of Moses and Aaron, the holy one of the LORD, the earth opened and swallowed up Dathan, and covered the company of Abiram."

213. **"Maddened heifer."** (Hosea 4:16a) "Like a stubborn heifer, Israel is stubborn."

   (Hosea 10:11) "Ephraim was a trained heifer that loved to thresh, and I spared her fair neck; but I will put Ephraim to the yoke." Ephraim was a son of Joseph and patriarch of a tribe of Israel.

   "From the nets rescue then thy life, gaining wings." (Psalm 124:7) "We have escaped as a bird from the snare of the fowlers; the snare is broken, and we have escaped!"

209. From the night I seek Thee early, O Lover of mankind: give me light, I pray Thee, and guide me in Thy commandments, and teach me, O Savior, to do Thy will.

CHAPTER 23

CANTICLE SIX

210. With my whole heart I cried to the all-compassionate God: and He heard me from the lowest depths of hell, and brought my life out of corruption.

Have mercy on me, O God, have mercy on me.

211. I offer to Thee in purity, O Savior, the tears of mine eyes and groanings from the depths of my heart, crying: "I have sinned against Thee, O God; be merciful to me."

Have mercy on me, O God, have mercy on me.

212. Like Dathan and Abiram, O my soul, thou hast become a stranger to Thy Lord; but with all thy heart cry out, "Spare me," that the earth may not open and swallow thee up.

Have mercy on me, O God, have mercy on me.

213. Raging as a maddened heifer, O my soul, thou art become like Ephraim. As a hart from the nets rescue then thy life, gaining wings through action and the mind's contemplation.

Have mercy on me, O God, have mercy on me.

214. **"The hand of Moses."** (Exodus 4:6-7) One of the signs by which the Lord proved Moses's authority to speak in His name. Moses' hand was made "leprous, white as snow" and then immediately healed.

215. **"The waters of the Red Sea engulfed the Egyptians."** (Exodus 14:21–28) When the Hebrews had safely crossed though the Red Sea, the Lord closed its waters again, drowning and destroying Pharaoh's pursuing army.

216. **"Instead of divine manna."** (Exodus 16:15) When the Hebrews were hungry in the wilderness, God provided food in the form of a fine, flake-like residue left on the ground after the morning dew evaporated. Manna means "What is it?"

(Exodus 16:14-15) "[W]hen the dew had gone up, there was on the face of the wilderness a fine, flake-like thing, fine as hoarfrost on the ground. When the people of Israel saw it, they said to one another, 'What is it?' For they did not know what it was. And Moses said to them, 'It is the bread which the LORD has given you to eat.'"

The people grew sick of manna. (Numbers 11:4–6) "[T]he people of Israel also wept again, and said, 'O that we had meat to eat! We remember the fish we ate in Egypt for nothing, the cucumbers, the melons, the leeks, the onions, and the garlic; but now our strength is dried up, and there is nothing at all but this manna to look at.'"

(Numbers 21:5) "[T]he people spoke against God and against Moses, 'Why have you brought us up out of Egypt to die in the wilderness? For there is no food and no water, and we loathe this worthless food.'"

(1 Corinthians 10:9-10a) "We must not put the Lord to the test, as some of them did . . . nor grumble."

CONSIDER

Verse 215 says, **"The waves of my sins have returned and suddenly engulfed me."** Have you experienced a sudden onslaught of temptation, and found it hard to resist? St. Andrew describes this experience as being like drowning in a collision of waves. Which sins are most likely to attack you with devastating suddenness?

In the Greek of the New Testament, "salvation" does not mean legal acquittal, but rescue, like being saved from drowning. Present your helplessness to the Lord, and ask Him to be your strength.

214. O my soul, the hand of Moses shall be our assurance, proving that God can cleanse a life full of leprosy and make it white as snow. So do not despair of thyself, though thou art leprous.

Have mercy on me, O God, have mercy on me.

215. The waves of my sins, O Savior, have returned and suddenly engulfed me, as the waters of the Red Sea engulfed the Egyptians of old and their charioteers.

Have mercy on me, O God, have mercy on me.

216. Like Israel before thee, thou hast made a foolish choice, my soul; instead of the divine manna thou hast senselessly preferred the pleasure-loving gluttony of the passions.

Have mercy on me, O God, have mercy on me.

217. The swine's meat, the flesh-pots, and the food of Egypt thou hast preferred, my soul, to the food of heaven, as the ungrateful people did of old in the wilderness.

Have mercy on me, O God, have mercy on me.

CHAPTER 24

EXPLORE

218. "The veined Rock." As the Hebrews wandered in the wilderness, seeking the land of Canaan, they had little water, and complained to Moses, "Is the LORD among us or not?" (Exodus 17:7a). God told Moses, "[T]ake in your hand the rod with which you struck the Nile, and go. Behold, I will stand before you there on the rock at Horeb; and you shall strike the rock, and water shall come out of it, that the people may drink" (Exodus 17:5-6). When Moses struck the rock abundant water gushed forth.

(1 Corinthians 10:3-4) The Hebrews in the desert "all ate the same supernatural food and all drank the same supernatural drink. For they drank from the supernatural Rock which followed them, and the Rock was Christ."

219. "He prefigured Thy life-giving side." In Exodus 17:6 God says, "I will stand before you there on the rock." God himself is struck to provide life-giving water. When Christ's side was pierced with a lance, "there came out blood and water" (John 19:34).

(2 Samuel 22:2-3), "David said, "The LORD is my rock, and my fortress, and my deliverer, my God, my rock, in whom I take refuge, my shield and the horn of my salvation, my stronghold and my refuge, my savior; Thou savest me from violence."

220. "Like Joshua . . . search and spy out." (Numbers 13:17–14:30) When the Hebrews arrived at Canaan, Moses selected men to go in and explore the land. These "spies" brought back a terrifying report, that the inhabitants of the land were giants who could not be defeated. The Hebrews recoiled in fear and were ready to turn and go back to Egypt. God declared that, for each of the forty days that the spies had spent searching the land of Canaan, the Hebrews would spend a year lost in the desert, until all that generation of adults were dead. Only Joshua and Caleb, who had maintained that the land could be taken, would survive to enter Canaan.

Forty years later, after the death of Moses, "Joshua the son of Nun sent two men secretly from Shittim as spies, saying, 'Go, view the land, especially Jericho'" (Joshua 2:1b).

221. "Joshua against Amalek." Amalek, a grandson of Esau, deceitfully attacked the Hebrews in the wilderness. Joshua destroyed Amalek and his army.

CHAPTER 24

218. O my soul, thou hast valued the wells of Canaanite thoughts more than the veined Rock, Jesus, the Fountain of wisdom from which flow the rivers of divine knowledge.

Have mercy on me, O God, have mercy on me.

219. When Thy servant Moses struck the rock with his rod, he prefigured Thy life-giving side, O Savior, from which we all draw the water of life.

Have mercy on me, O God, have mercy on me.

220. Like Joshua the son of Nun, search and spy out, my soul, the land of thine inheritance and take up thy dwelling within it, through obedience to the law.

Have mercy on me, O God, have mercy on me.

221. Rise up and make war against the passions of the flesh, as Joshua against Amalek, ever gaining the victory over the Gibeonites, thy deceitful thoughts.

Have mercy on me, O God, have mercy on me.

(Deuteronomy 25:17–19) "Remember what Amalek did to you on the way as you came out of Egypt, how he attacked you on the way, when you were faint and weary, and cut off at your rear all who lagged behind you; and he did not fear God. Therefore . . . you shall blot out the remembrance of Amalek from under heaven."

"The Gibeonites." (Joshua 9:3–27) When Joshua began to conquer Canaan, most inhabitants of the land united to oppose him. But a tribe called the Gibeonites instead made a clever plan. Representatives came to Joshua, dressed in worn-out clothing and carrying moldy provisions, asking for a covenant of peace. Joshua's men were suspicious and asked whether they lived nearby, but the Gibeonites showed their broken sandals and dried-out wineskins as evidence that they had come from far away. Only after the agreement was struck did the Hebrews learn that they had been duped into guaranteeing peace to a people who lived in their midst.

222. **"The ark of old."** Not the ark of Noah, the ship that survived the flood, but the ark of the covenant, which was carried across the Jordan with Joshua when he entered Canaan. As the priests carrying the ark touched the brink of the Jordan, all the waters "rose up in a heap" and the people passed over on dry land, as at the Red Sea. (Joshua 3:17) "[W]hile all Israel were passing over on dry ground, the priests who bore the ark of the covenant of the LORD stood on dry ground in the midst of the Jordan."

"Take possession of the land of promise." (Deuteronomy 1:8) "[G]o in and take possession of the land which the LORD swore to your fathers, to Abraham, to Isaac, and to Jacob, to give to them and to their descendants after them."

223. **"Peter . . . cried out, 'Save me.'"** (Matthew 14:30-31) Peter was sinking in the waves.

"Save me from the beast." The Beast is seen in a vision by Daniel (Daniel 7:2–27) and by St. John (Revelation 13:1–18).

CONSIDER

The trick of the Gibeonites is a clever one. St. Andrew says that we play such tricks on ourselves, when we persuade ourselves that the things our passions urge us toward are not really sinful.

Western culture places highest trust in the capability of the logical mind. We assume that "reason" leads us to truth. But our ability to reason is infected with passions and misperceptions. A thread of logical argument may make impeccable sense, but it

100

222. O my soul, pass through the flowing waters of time like the ark of old, and take possession of the land of promise, for God commands thee.

Have mercy on me, O God, have mercy on me.

223. As Thou hast saved Peter when he cried out, "Save me," come quickly, O Savior, before it is too late, and save me from the beast. Stretch out Thine hand and lead me up from the deep of sin.

Have mercy on me, O God, have mercy on me.

224. I know Thee as a calm haven, O Lord, Lord Christ: come quickly, before it is too late, and deliver me from the lowest depths of sin and despair.

Have mercy on me, O God, have mercy on me.

might be undermined by a missing bit of information (as was the case with the Gibeonites), or even by self-deception. There is a reason that the word "rational" is related to the word "rationalize." Which sins are you most likely to rationalize away, deceiving yourself as the Gibeonites deceived Joshua?

COMMENTARY
CHAPTER 25

EXPLORE

225. **"The coin . . . which Thou hast lost."** (Luke 15:8–10) "[W]hat woman, having ten silver coins, if she loses one coin, does not light a lamp and sweep the house and seek diligently until she finds it? And when she has found it, she calls together her friends and neighbors, saying, 'Rejoice with me, for I have found the coin which I had lost.' Just so, I tell you, there is joy before the angels of God over one sinner who repents."

"Marked with the king's likeness." In the ancient world, a coin usually bore a portrait of the king or emperor of that land.

(Genesis 1:26a) "Then God said, 'Let us make man in our image, after our likeness.'"

"Thy lamp, Thy Forerunner." In John 5:35 Jesus describes St. John the Forerunner: "He was a burning and shining lamp, and you were willing to rejoice for a while in his light." (In the Eastern Church, St. John is usually called "the Forerunner," rather than "the Baptist.") (Mark 1:2) "Behold, I send my messenger before thy face, who shall prepare thy way."

228. **"Deliver me, father, from the depths of sin."** (Psalm 130:1-2) "Out of the depths I cry to thee, O LORD! LORD, hear my voice! Let thine ears be attentive to the voice of my supplications!"

(Micah 7:19b) "Thou wilt cast all our sins into the depths of the sea."

CHAPTER 25

225. O Savior, I am the coin marked with the King's likeness, which Thou hast lost of old. But, O Word, light Thy lamp, Thy forerunner, and seek and find again Thine image.

Holy Mother Mary, pray to God for us.

226. Thy soul on fire, O Mary, thou hast ever shed streams of tears, to quench the burning of the passions. Grant the grace of these thy tears to me also, thy servant.

Holy Mother Mary, pray to God for us.

227. Through the perfection of thine earthly life, O Mother, thou hast gained a heavenly freedom from the sinfulness of passion. In thine intercessions pray that this same freedom may be given to those who sing thy praises.

Holy Father Andrew, pray to God for us.

228. Shepherd and bishop of Crete, intercessor for the inhabited earth, to thee I run, O Andrew, and I cry: "Deliver me, father, from the depths of sin."

Glory to the Father, and to the Son, and to the Holy Spirit.

230. **"That we may be justified through thine intercessions."** This prayer does not make sense if we understand "justified" in the usual Western Christian way, as meaning the legal pardon of the debt for our sins. Instead, "justified" here means being brought into right order with our Father, the Creator of all. It is a relationship problem, not a legal problem. Recall the earlier analogies to God's presence being like fire. We are "justified" when we, through humility and repentance, have been changed to be like Him, and to be able to bear His fire. We ask the Virgin Theotokos to pray for us, so that our hearts, softened by repentance, will be conformed to God's presence and made harmonious with His will.

232. In the sung service of the Great Canon, several hours have already passed; the chanting lifts the worshiper to a place of quietly subdued reflection which seems beyond the reach of time. Then this verse breaks through. It is a rousing cry: **"Rise up! Why are you sleeping?"**

(Mark 13:35–37) "Watch therefore—for you do not know when the master of the house will come, in the evening, or at midnight, or at cockcrow, or in the morning—lest he come suddenly and find you asleep. And what I say to you I say to all: Watch."

"Everywhere present and fills all things."—This phrase concludes the prayer to the Holy Spirit, used in most Orthodox services.

(Jeremiah 23:24) "Can a man hide himself in secret places so that I cannot see him? says the LORD. Do I not fill heaven and earth? says the LORD."

(Psalm 139:7–10) "Whither shall I go from thy Spirit? Or whither shall I flee from thy presence? If I ascend to heaven, thou art there! If I make my bed in Sheol, thou art there! If I take the wings of the morning and dwell in the uttermost parts of the sea, even there thy hand shall lead me, and thy right hand shall hold me."

233. **"Christ's house of healing opened, and health flows down from it upon Adam."** Christ was crucified at Golgotha, which means in Hebrew "the place of the skull." Icons show Christ's blood flowing down to anoint a skull at the base of the cross—the skull of Adam.

The devil's lamenting at Christ's resurrection power is a recurrent theme in the services of Holy Week. In the compline service of the Friday night before Palm Sunday, Christ is seen calling Lazarus back to life, and this throws the devil into a panic. "'I implore thee, Lazarus,' said Hades, 'rise up, depart quickly from my bonds and

229. "I am the Trinity, simple and undivided, yet divided in Persons, and I am the Unity, by nature one," says the Father, and the Son, and the divine Spirit.

Both now and ever and unto ages of ages. Amen.

230. Thy womb bore God for us, fashioned in our shape. O Theotokos, pray to Him as the Creator of all, that we may be justified through thine intercessions.

231. With my whole heart I cried to the all-compassionate God, and He heard me from the lowest depths of hell, and brought my life out of corruption.

232. My soul, O my soul, rise up! Why art thou sleeping? The end draws near, and soon thou shalt be troubled. Watch, then, that Christ thy God may spare thee, for He is everywhere present and fills all things.

233. Seeing Christ's house of healing opened, and health flowing down from it upon Adam, the devil suffered and was wounded; and as one in mortal danger he lamented, crying to his friends: "What shall I do to the Son of Mary? I am slain by the Man from Bethlehem, who is everywhere present and fills all things."

be gone. It is better for me to lament bitterly for the loss of one, rather than of all those whom I have swallowed in my hunger.'"

CONSIDER

"I am the coin marked by the king's likeness." We live in a visual age; we are surrounded by billboards, magazine covers, television, and movies. Instead of reading newspapers, we watch the twenty-four-hour news channel. Instead of reading novels, we watch movies.

A side effect is that we are surrounded by images of people who appear unnaturally beautiful. (Their beauty is indeed unnatural.) This contributes to an increased anxiety about appearances. We are constantly reminded of the correct way to look, and we see how far we fall short every time we glance in a mirror.

Yet we are **"marked by the king's likeness."** No matter how humble our physical appearance, we bear the imprint of our Creator inside. And no matter how much we have smeared and soiled our souls, we retain the indelible image of God.

A lost coin can't find itself; it can't even cry out for help. But our Lord lights His lamp and comes searching for us. Reflect on the indelible image of God retained in your being, despite your imperfections and sins, and on Christ's search to recover you for His own.

COMMENTARY
CHAPTER 26

EXPLORE

The Beatitudes. When Jesus saw that the crowds were surrounding Him, He went up on a mountain where He was joined by His disciples. There He delivered a series of teachings, called "The Sermon on the Mount," which fill chapters five through seven of the Gospel of Matthew. The opening verses of this sermon, Matthew 5:3–11, are commonly called "the Beatitudes," a word meaning "the blessings." Each verse begins, "Blessed are. . . ."

Here, between Canticle Six and Canticle Seven, we pause for the Beatitudes, which become the responses in this section in place of "Have mercy on me, O God." The first line is derived from the words of the good thief on the cross: "Jesus, remember me when you come into your kingly power" (Luke 23:42).

234. **"Grant me to repent like him."** Even repentance is not a work that we can undertake on our own. We must pray to be delivered

106

CHAPTER 26

THE BEATITUDES

In Thy Kingdom remember us, O Lord,
when Thou comest in Thy Kingdom.

234. O Christ, when the thief cried to Thee upon the cross
"Remember me," Thou hast made him a citizen of
Paradise. Unworthy though I am, grant me to repent
like him.

Blessed are the poor in spirit,
for theirs is the kingdom of heaven.

from fear and confusion, and enabled to see the truth about ourselves and offer it to God for healing.

235.   **"Manoah beheld the Lord in a vision."** (Judges 13:2–25) St. Andrew continues his pilgrimage through the Old Testament. Manoah was the father of Samson. His wife was barren, but she had a vision in which an angel told her that she would conceive a son. (The understanding of the early Christians was that any appearance of "an angel of the Lord" in the Old Testament is an appearance of Christ Himself.) Later, Manoah saw this angel as well. When he asked its name he received the reply, "Why do you ask my name, seeing it is wonderful?" (Judges 13:18).

236.   **"Samson's slothfulness."** The Philistines threatened Samson's wife, Delilah, demanding that she tell them the secret of his great strength. When he was worn down by her incessant pleading, he finally confessed that it was because he had never cut his hair, in obedience to a vow his parents had made before he was born. Then, while Samson was sleeping, Delilah had his hair shorn, and he was made helpless. The Philistines put his eyes out and brought him in chains to grind at a mill.

237.   **"Overthrew the Philistines with the jawbone of an ass."** (Judges 15:14–16) An earlier attempt of the Philistines to capture Samson failed, when he broke through the bonds that held him and started swinging at them with his only weapon, the jawbone of a dead donkey he found lying nearby. "With the jawbone of an ass, heaps upon heaps, with the jawbone of an ass have I slain a thousand men."

238.   **"Barak and Jephthah, with Deborah."** Barak (Judges 4:6–5:15) and Jephthah (Judges 11:1–12:7) were military captains, and Deborah (Judges 4:4–5:15) was a judge over Israel, in the early years of settlement in Canaan before Israel had a monarchy.

239.   **"Manly courage of Jael."** (Judges 4:17–22). Barak was fighting for Israel against Jabin, king of Canaan. Jabin's general, Sisera, fled from Barak and took shelter in the tent of the wife of one of Jabin's allies, a woman named Jael. She covered him with a rug and gave him milk to drink, then encouraged him to rest. While he was sleeping, Jael "took a tent peg, and took a hammer in her hand, and went softly to him and drove the peg into his temple, till it went down into the ground."

In this way Jael saved Israel by a hammer and nail, an act which St. Andrew says prefigures our own salvation by the nails of the cross.

235. O my soul, thou hast heard how Manoah of old beheld the Lord in a vision, and then received from his barren wife the fruit of God's promise. Let us imitate him in his devotion.

Blessed are they that mourn,
for they shall be comforted.

236. Emulating Samson's slothfulness, O my soul, thou hast been shorn of the glory of thy works, and through love of pleasure thou hast betrayed thy life to the alien Philistines, surrendering thy chastity and blessedness.

Blessed are the meek,
for they shall inherit the earth.

237. He who at the first overthrew the Philistines with the jawbone of an ass, then wasted his life in passionate lusts. Flee, O my soul, from his example, flee from his actions and his weakness.

Blessed are they that hunger and thirst
after righteousness, for they shall be filled.

238. Barak and Jepthah the captains, with Deborah who had a man's courage, were chosen as judges of Israel. Learn bravery from their mighty acts, O my soul, and be strong.

Blessed are the merciful, for they shall obtain mercy.

239. O my soul, thou knowest the manly courage of Jael, who of old pierced Sisera through his temples and

240. **"Daughter of Jephthah."** The military captain Jephthah (Judges 11:1–12:7) made a foolish and horrifying vow; he said that, if given victory in battle, he would sacrifice to God whoever came out to greet him when he returned home. "[A]nd behold, his daughter came out to meet him with timbrels and with dances; she was his only child; beside her he had neither son nor daughter." Jephthah was stricken. "And when he saw her, he rent his clothes, and said, 'Alas, my daughter! You have brought me very low, and you have become the cause of great trouble to me; for I have opened my mouth to the LORD, and I cannot take back my vow'" (Judges 11:34-35). The daughter agreed to abide by this vow, asking only to be given two months to mourn, a custom that continued among the daughters of Israel.

CONSIDER

The verses in this section cover a time in the history of Israel that seems very remote to us, in its brutality and violence. Samson was a man of blood who boasted of destroying thousands, and he himself was attacked and forcibly blinded. Jael murdered Sisera in a valiant but gruesome manner. The sacrifice of Jephthah's daughter is appalling. And in the beginning of this section we see three men, nailed through the hands and feet, streaming with blood, suspended on wooden crosses.

The idea of nailing a person to a cross fails to shock us as it should, because we have grown used to it. It's not accurate to call this form of execution "barbaric"; very civilized Romans thought it through carefully. They needed a form of punishment in which the criminal would be quite literally held up as an example. It needed to be a means which would defile the body, as after death it would hang in reach of pecking birds and gnawing beasts. That way no burial place could comfort the family or become a rallying point for rebels. It needed to be a means that would not be swift, so the message would be memorable; crucifixion usually took days, unless the criminal's legs were broken and he could no longer brace his weight to draw a breath.

There can be few forms of torture as inventively cruel as a crucifixion. It recalls the kind of newspaper story you can read and then wish you had never read, which reveals more about the capacity of humans for hideous cruelty than you ever suspected.

brought salvation to Israel with the nail of her tent. In this thou mayest see a prefiguring of the Cross.

Blessed are the pure in heart,
for they shall see God.

240. Offer, my soul, a sacrifice worthy of praise, offer thine actions as an oblation purer than the daughter of Jepthah; and as a victim for thy Lord slay the passions of the flesh.

Blessed are the peacemakers,
for they shall be called the children of God.

And yet that very instrument of torture is what God accepted, and then used against the evil one. The ugliest thing the devil could devise explodes in his hands. He lost control of his nasty invention. This weapon of shame and horror becomes an implement of radiant victory, and Christians everywhere take it up, and wear crosses, and sign themselves with the cross—this thing the evil one invented, to wreak misery and death!

We think that fighting evil looks like using earthly force and power, like Samson and Jael and Jephthah. But Christ saved the whole world by enduring death. The cross became a throne.

COMMENTARY
CHAPTER 27

EXPLORE

241. **"Fleece of Gideon."** (Judges 6:36–40) Gideon asked for a sign that God would make him victorious in battle. He placed a fleece on the threshing floor, and prayed that in the morning the fleece would be wet with dew, while the ground was dry. (Judges 6:38) "And it was so. When he rose early next morning and squeezed the fleece, he wrung enough dew from the fleece to fill a bowl with water."

"Bend down like a hart and drink." (Psalm 42:1) "As a hart longs for flowing streams, so longs my soul for thee, O God." There is also a suggestion of Judges 7:5–7: God told Gideon that his army was too large, and that Israel might think they won the battle by their own hand rather than God's strength. God told Gideon to have his men drink from a stream; all who bent down to drink were set aside, and only those who cupped their hands to drink were allowed to fight.

242. **"Condemnation of Eli the priest."** (1 Samuel 2:12–25) Eli's sons, Hophni and Phinehas, demanded portions from the offerings brought by worshipers, and slept with women who served at the entrance of the tent of meeting. They ignored their father's corrections, and he gave up trying to discipline them.

243. **"The Levite divided his wife limb from limb."** (Judges 19:15–30) Another appalling story from the Old Testament. A Levite and his concubine, traveling through the land of the Benjaminites, were given shelter by an old man. In a scene reminiscent of the story of Lot in Sodom, men of the city

112

CHAPTER 27

241. O my soul, consider the fleece of Gideon, and receive the dew from heaven; bend down like a hart and drink the water that flows from the Law, when its letter is wrung out for thee through study.

Blessed are they that are persecuted for righteousness' sake, for theirs is the kingdom of heaven.

242. Thou hast drawn upon thyself, O my soul, the condemnation of Eli the priest: thoughtlessly thou hast allowed the passions to work evil within thee, just as he permitted his children to commit transgressions.

Blessed are ye, when men shall revile you, and persecute you, and shall say all manner of evil against you falsely, for My sake.

243. In the book of Judges, my soul, the Levite divided his wife limb from limb and sent the parts to the twelve tribes; and so he made known the lawless outrage committed by the men of Benjamin.

surrounded the house and demanded that the Levite be brought out "that we may know [i.e., rape] him." The Levite thrust his concubine (wife) outside instead, and the men raped and abused her till dawn. She made it back to the house, but fell exhausted and died with her hands on the threshold of the door. In the morning her master saw what had happened, and cut her into twelve pieces and sent them throughout the territory of Israel, as evidence of the evil the Benjaminites had done.

244. **"Hannah . . . moved her lips in praise."** (1 Samuel 1:1–20) Hannah was barren, and every year on her annual trip to worship at the temple she would pray that she would bear a son. One year the priest Eli (verse 242) noticed her there, apparently mumbling to herself. (1 Samuel 1:13) "Hannah was speaking in her heart; only her lips moved, and her voice was not heard." Eli rebuked her, thinking she was drunk, but she explained that she was praying for a child. He told her that her prayer was granted, and in due time she had a son, Samuel.

245. **"Great Samuel . . . brought up in the house of the Lord."** (1 Samuel 1:27-28) Hannah had vowed that, if God gave her a son, she would "lend" him back. When Samuel had been weaned she brought him to the temple and left him in Eli's care. "As long as he lives, he is lent to the LORD," she said. She made the child a new robe every year and brought it to him on her visits, and filled her home with more sons and daughters. Samuel became one of Israel's greatest judges, and anointed both Saul and David as king.

246. **"David was chosen to be king and anointed."** (1 Samuel 16:13) "Then Samuel took the horn of oil, and anointed him in the midst of his brothers; and the Spirit of the LORD came mightily upon David from that day forward." Both "Messiah" in Hebrew and "Christ" in Greek mean "Anointed One."

CONSIDER

"Have mercy on Thy creation, merciful Lord." "Remember us, when Thou comest in Thy kingdom." Many of these examples show people being apparently rewarded or punished for their deeds. Yet it is not God's will that anyone suffer; His plan is for all to be with Him in His kingdom.

The eloquent fourth-century bishop St. John Chrysostom invites us to take a closer look at Jesus' parable of the sheep and

Rejoice and be exceeding glad, for great is your
reward in heaven.

244. Hannah, who loved self-restraint and chastity, when speaking to God moved her lips in praise, but her voice was not heard; and she who was barren bore a son worthy of her prayer.

Remember us, O Lord,
when Thou comest in Thy kingdom.

245. Great Samuel, the son of Hannah, was born at Ramah and brought up in the house of the Lord; and he was numbered among the judges of Israel. Eagerly follow his example, O my soul, and before thou judgest others, judge thine own works.

Remember us, O Master,
when Thou comest in Thy kingdom.

246. David was chosen to be king and anointed for his royal office with the horn of divine oil. If thou, my soul, desirest the kingdom on high, anoint thyself with the oil of tears.

Remember us, O Holy One,
when Thou comest in Thy kingdom.

247. Have mercy upon Thy creation, merciful Lord; take pity on the work of Thy hands. Spare those who have sinned, and spare me who more than all others have despised Thy commandments.

Glory to the Father, and to the Son, and
to the Holy Spirit.

248. Without beginning are the birth of the Son and the procession of the Spirit. I worship the Father who

the goats in Matthew 25. The beginning of the story is familiar: (Matthew 25:31-46) "When the Son of man comes in his glory, and all the angels with him, then he will sit on his glorious throne. Before him will be gathered all the nations, and he will separate them one from another as a shepherd separates the sheep from the goats." To those on His right He will say, "Come, O blessed of my Father, inherit the kingdom prepared for you from the foundation of the world." But those on the left will hear, "Depart from me, you cursed, into the eternal fire prepared for the devil and his angels."

St. John points out that what is prepared for humanity is a kingdom; God's will and intention is that we come and be with Him. The "eternal fire" is not prepared for us, but for "the devil and his angels." (Note, too, that the devil does not rule over hell and torment humans; rather, the devil is confined in hell to suffer.)

Eternal suffering is not God's plan for any child of Adam and Eve. We fail to enter the kingdom because of our own choices, and in spite of the urgency of God's mercy and His continual attempts to draw us back. Pray today for those who are far from God, and who cannot perceive His mercy.

COMMENTARY
CHAPTER 28

EXPLORE

250. The *irmos* of Canticle Seven echoes the seventh biblical canticle, the Song of Azariah. In the third chapter of the book of Daniel, King Nebuchadnezzar had an immense golden statue of himself made, and commanded all his people to fall down and worship it. Daniel's three companions, Shadrach, Meshach, and Abednego (their Hebrew names are Hannaniah, Mishael, and Azariah), refused to do so. The king had them thrown into a "burning fiery furnace," but instead of being destroyed, they stood up and sang two hymns of praise to God. This passage appears in the Septuagint version of Daniel, at 3:26–56. (It does not appear in most Western Bibles, though it may be included in an appendix titled "Apocrypha.")

The first hymn, the Song of Azariah, is a prayer of repentance. "We have sinned and have transgressed . . . Thy commandments have we not heard . . . Deliver us not up utterly, for Thy holy

begets, I glorify the Son who is begotten, and I sing the praises of the Holy Spirit who shines forth with the Father and the Son.

Both now and ever and unto ages of ages. Amen.

249. O Mother of God, we venerate thy childbearing in ways past nature, yet we do not divide in two the natural glory of thy Son: for He is confessed as one Person in two Natures.

CHAPTER 28

CANTICLE SEVEN

250. We have sinned, we have transgressed, we have done evil in Thy sight; we have not kept or followed Thy commandments. But reject us not utterly, O God of our fathers.

Have mercy on me, O God, have mercy on me.

251. I have sinned, I have offended, I have set aside Thy commandments; for in sins have I progressed and to my sores I have added wounds. But in Thy compassion have mercy upon me, O God of our fathers.

Have mercy on me, O God, have mercy on me.

name's sake." Israel has been defeated and enslaved by the Babylonians. Rather than protesting this, Azariah acknowledges that it is due to the people's sins.

252. **"The secrets of my heart."** (Psalm 90:8) "Thou hast set our iniquities before thee, our secret sins in the light of thy countenance."

(Ecclesiastes 12:14) "For God will bring every deed into judgment, with every secret thing, whether good or evil."

(Psalm 51:6) "Behold, thou desirest truth in the inward being; therefore teach me wisdom in my secret heart."

253. **"Saul lost his father's asses."** (1 Samuel 9:3–10:9) The young Saul went out to search for some of his father's asses that had gone astray. When he didn't find them, his servant recommended that they go to a nearby town and ask the seer who lived there—the prophet Samuel. Samuel anointed Saul king over Israel.

254. **"David . . . sinned doubly."** (2 Samuel 11:2–17) David took Bathsheba, the beautiful young wife of a soldier at the battlefront, and slept with her. When she notified David that she was pregnant, David had her husband, Uriah, called home, and sent him to be with his wife. Uriah nobly replied that he would not partake of any comforts unavailable to his fellow soldiers, and slept at the door of the king's house. David then sent a message to his general by Uriah's hand, to put the soldier in the fiercest part of the battle and then suddenly pull back, leaving him defenseless. Uriah was killed.

255. **"Yet he at once showed a twofold repentance."** (2 Samuel 12:1–13) The prophet Nathan came to David with a story of a wealthy man, owner of vast flocks, who stole the pet lamb of a poor man and slaughtered it to feed a guest. When David angrily declared "[T]he man who has done this deserves to die," Nathan responded, "You are the man." David said, "I have sinned against the LORD."

256. **"David once composed a hymn."** David's psalm of repentance is Psalm 51.

(Psalm 51:2–4) "Wash me thoroughly from my iniquity, and cleanse me from my sin! For I know my transgressions, and my sin is ever before me. Against thee, thee only, have I sinned, and done that which is evil in thy sight, so that thou art justified in thy sentence and blameless in thy judgment."

252. The secrets of my heart have I confessed to Thee, my Judge. See my abasement, see my affliction, and attend to my judgment now; and in Thy compassion have mercy upon me, O God of our fathers.

Have mercy on me, O God, have mercy on me.

253. When Saul once lost his father's asses, in searching for them he found himself proclaimed as king. But watch, my soul, lest unknown to thyself thou prefer thine animal appetites to the kingdom of Christ.

Have mercy on me, O God, have mercy on me.

254. David, the forefather of God, once sinned doubly, pierced with the arrow of adultery and the spear of murder. But thou, my soul, art more gravely sick than he, for worse than any acts are the impulses of thy will.

Have mercy on me, O God, have mercy on me.

255. David once joined sin to sin, adding murder to fornication; yet then he showed at once a twofold repentance. But thou, my soul, hast done worse things than he, yet thou hast not repented before God.

Have mercy on me, O God, have mercy on me.

256. David once composed a hymn, setting forth, as in an icon, the action he had done; and he condemned it, crying: "Have mercy upon me, for against Thee only have I sinned, O God of all. Do Thou cleanse me."

Have mercy on me, O God, have mercy on me.

257. **"Uzzah did no more than touch it."** When David was bringing the ark of the covenant to Jerusalem on an oxcart, the driver put out his hand to steady it and was suddenly struck dead. (2 Samuel 6:6-7) "Uzzah put out his hand to the ark of God and took hold of it, for the oxen stumbled. And the anger of the LORD was kindled against Uzzah; and God smote him there because he put forth his hand to the ark; and he died there beside the ark of God."

258. **"Absalom . . . defiled his father David's bed."** Absalom challenged his father for leadership of Israel. In a deliberately outrageous gesture, he had a tent pitched on a rooftop and brought in his father's concubines publicly, so that this insult would be known. Nathan had predicted many years before that this would be part of David's punishment for his sin against Uriah. (2 Samuel 12:11-12) "Behold, I will raise up evil against you out of your own house; and I will take your wives before your eyes, and give them to your neighbor, and he shall lie with your wives in the sight of this sun. For you did it secretly; but I will do this thing before all Israel, and before the sun."

CONSIDER

The Israelites always knew to turn to God in repentance when disaster struck. When they were defeated and enslaved by Babylon and carried away in captivity, their response, as we see in the Song of Azariah, was to admit that their own sins provoked this chastisement.

We react in the opposite way today. When misfortune strikes we think, "How dare God allow this to happen?" We blame Him for not preventing it; we think that He is cruel and capricious. Some pastors even urge parishioners to express anger at God. But this is wholly contrary to the pattern in Scripture. There we learn that, if God's patient forebearance fails to cause His people to return to Him, then He will use misfortune. As Azariah would say, "In truth and judgment hast Thou brought all these things upon us for our sins."

These tragic events are not simple tit for tat punishments, but disciplines, teaching tools. They aim to strip a person of self-satisfaction and cause him to return to God in humility. However, some tragedies spring from the malice of the evil one, who hates all humankind. (Matthew 13:28) "An enemy has done this." His power to inflict such evil is supported by human sin,

257. When the ark was being carried in a cart and the ox stumbled, Uzzah did no more than touch it, but the wrath of God smote him. O my soul, flee from his presumption and respect with reverence the things of God.

Have mercy on me, O God, have mercy on me.

258. Thou hast heard of Absalom, and how he rebelled against nature; thou knowest of the unholy deeds by which he defiled his father, David's bed. Yet thou hast followed him in his passionate and sensual desires.

Have mercy on me, O God, have mercy on me.

which runs like poison through the world. When children and the innocent suffer it is especially sweet for the evil one, because he can enjoy both the pain they endure and also the grief and confusion we onlookers feel—we, whose petty lies, gossiping, and anger built up his strength in the first place.

It is not up to us to figure out why a tragedy happened. We only have to respond to it—casting ourselves on the mercy of God, searching our hearts in repentance, and abandoning ourselves wholly to Him.

COMMENTARY

CHAPTER 29

EXPLORE

259. **"Another Ahitophel."** (2 Samuel 16:20-21) Ahitophel was a counselor highly respected by both David and his rebellious son Absalom. (2 Samuel 16:23) "Now in those days the counsel which Ahithophel gave was as if one consulted the oracle of God." Ahithophel gave Absalom the advice that he have sex with his father's concubines in public view.

260. **"Solomon . . . did evil in the sight of heaven."** As a young king, Solomon had pleased God by asking for wisdom instead of riches or longevity. But he had an insatiable craving for women, and among his thousand wives and concubines were those whom the Israelites were forbidden to marry because they worshiped other gods. (1 Kings 11:4) "[W]hen Solomon was old his wives turned away his heart after other gods; and his heart was not wholly true to the LORD his God, as was the heart of David his father."

261. To please his wives, Solomon built temples for foreign gods, even those who demanded human sacrifice. (1 Kings 11:5–8) "For Solomon went after Ashtoreth the goddess of the Sidonians, and after Milcom the abomination of the Ammonites. . . . [He] built a high place for Chemosh the abomination of Moab, and for Molech the abomination of the Ammonites, on the mountain east of Jerusalem. And so he did for all his foreign wives, who burned incense and sacrificed to their gods."

CHAPTER 29

259. Thy free dignity, O my soul, thou hast subjected to thy body; for thou hast found in the enemy another Ahitophel, and hast agreed to all his counsels. But Christ Himself has brought them to nothing and saved thee from them all.

Have mercy on me, O God, have mercy on me.

260. Solomon the wonderful, who was full of the grace of wisdom, once did evil in the sight of heaven and turned away from God. Thou hast become like him, my soul, through thine accursed life.

Have mercy on me, O God, have mercy on me.

261. Carried away by sensual passions, he defiled himself. Alas! The lover of wisdom became a lover of harlots and a stranger to God. And thou, my soul, in thy mind hast imitated him through thy shameful desires.

Have mercy on me, O God, have mercy on me.

262. **"Rehoboam, who paid no attention . . . Jeroboam, that evil servant."** (1 Kings 11:26–12:33). Rehoboam, the son of Solomon, became king in his place. Jeroboam was a servant of Solomon, but the prophet Ahijah told him that, as punishment for Solomon's betrayal of the faith, God was going to take away most of Rehoboam's kingdom, and give ten of the twelve tribes to Jeroboam. Early in Rehoboam's reign, Jeroboam came to the new king seeking better treatment for his people. Solomon's aged counselors urged Rehoboam to agree to this, but hot-headed young advisers told Rehoboam to treat them yet more harshly.

263. **"Rivaled Ahab in guilt."** King Ahab and his wife, Jezebel, rejected the faith of Israel in favor of foreign gods, Baal and Ashtoreth. (1 Kings 16:33) "Ahab did more to provoke the LORD, the God of Israel, to anger than all the kings of Israel who were before him."

264. **"Elijah destroyed."** (1 Kings 18:18–40) The prophet Elijah continually rebuked Ahab and Jezebel. In a contest to show the strength of their gods, Elijah and the 450 prophets of Baal each prepared a sacrifice, and each prayed that God would send fire from heaven to set it alight. The prophets of Baal performed ceremonies till they were exhausted, but nothing happened. Elijah prepared an altar and soaked it in water, and at his prayer fire came down and consumed the offering, and even licked up all the water in the surrounding ditch. The 450 prophets of Baal were slain.

Ahaziah, Ahab's son, was similarly rebellious against God. He sent fifty servants to ask a word of Elijah, and they were consumed by fire from heaven. He sent fifty more with a sterner request, and they met the same fate. A third appeal, phrased more humbly, won Elijah's agreement to speak to the king (2 Kings 1:9–16).

265. **"Heaven is closed to thee."** (1 Kings 17:1) "Elijah the Tishbite, of Tishbe in Gilead, said to Ahab, 'As the LORD the God of Israel lives, before whom I stand, there shall be neither dew nor rain these years, except by my word.'" After speaking these words Elijah fled and hid in the desert, then was told by God to go to the town of Zarephath.

(1 Kings 17:9) "Behold, I have commanded a widow there to feed you." The widow was impoverished, but while Elijah remained with her, her flour and oil never gave out. When her son died, Elijah prayed and God restored him to life.

Jesus used this woman as an example of God's favor on people outside the bounds of Israel. (Luke 4:25-26) "I tell you, there were many widows in Israel in the days of Elijah, when the heaven was

262. O my soul, thou hast rivaled Rehoboam, who paid no attention to his father's counselors, and Jeroboam, that evil servant and renegade of old. But flee from their example and cry to God: I have sinned, take pity on me.

Have mercy on me, O God, have mercy on me.

263. Alas, my soul! Thou hast rivaled Ahab in guilt. Thou hast become the dwelling-place of fleshly defilements and a shameful vessel of the passions. But groan from the depths of thy heart, and confess thy sins to God.

Have mercy on me, O God, have mercy on me.

264. Elijah once destroyed with fire twice fifty of Jezebel's servants, and he slew the prophets of shame, as a rebuke to Ahab. But flee from the example of both of them, my soul, and be strong.

Have mercy on me, O God, have mercy on me.

265. Heaven is closed to thee, my soul, and a famine from God has seized thee: for thou hast been disobedient, as Ahab was to the words of Elijah the Tishbite. But imitate the widow of Zarephath, and feed the prophet's soul.

Have mercy on me, O God, have mercy on me.

shut up three years and six months, when there came a great famine over all the land; and Elijah was sent to none of them but only to Zarephath, in the land of Sidon, to a woman who was a widow."

266. **"Guilt of Manasseh."** Manasseh, king of Judah, undid many of the reforms of his father, Hezekiah, rebuilding altars to foreign gods, and burning his own sons as offerings. (2 Kings 21:9) "Manasseh seduced [the people] to do more evil than the nations had done whom the LORD destroyed before the people of Israel."

Yet when he was conquered and taken in chains to Babylon he repented. (2 Chronicles 33:12-13) "[W]hen he was in distress he entreated the favor of the LORD his God and humbled himself greatly before the God of his fathers. He prayed to him, and God received his entreaty and heard his supplication and brought him again to Jerusalem into his kingdom. Then Manasseh knew that the LORD was God."

"The Prayer of Manasseh" is found in the Septuagint, and is a beautiful hymn of repentance, like Psalm 51. "Surely Thou, O Lord, the God of the just, hast not appointed repentance for the just, for Abraham and Isaac and Jacob, who have not sinned against Thee. But Thou hast appointed repentance for me a sinner, for I have sinned above the number of the sand of the sea."

CONSIDER

In these Old Testament passages we find God closely involved in the details of life. He decrees that it will not rain for three years; He intervenes in the rise and fall of rulers; He places food inside the jars of the widow of Zarephath. He attends to this earth so closely that not a sparrow falls to the ground apart from his will (Matthew 10:29). "[E]ven the hairs of your head are all numbered" (Matthew 10:30).

Yet when we hear of someone who prays, for example, that God will help her find a parking place, we're offended. We think that God is too big to be bothered with such silly details. The reverse is true: We are the ones treating God in a silly, childish way. We are picturing Him as an oversized human being. We presume His mind is as limited as ours, and that He only has the capacity to deal with "really important" things.

126

266. By deliberate choice, my soul, thou hast incurred the guilt of Manasseh, setting up the passions as idols and multiplying abominations. But with fervent heart emulate his repentance and acquire compunction.

Have mercy on me, O God, have mercy on me.

But God is attending to and managing every tiny detail of life simultaneously. He is not outside creation, remote on a cloud, but filling it from the inside. "Do I not fill heaven and earth? says the LORD" (Jeremiah 23:24b). God is much more than earthly creation, but everything in it is filled with Him. God is Life. Nothing exists apart from Him. He sees inside the cupboard of a widow, sees inside her flour jar, and in that tiny space creates abundance where there was nothing. When God wants to count the hairs of your head, He can do it from the inside. What sense is there in trying to conceal anything from Him—your sins, or your needs?

COMMENTARY
CHAPTER 30

EXPLORE

267.　**"Sinned as the harlot never sinned."** (Luke 7:36–50) Jesus had been invited to dinner with a Pharisee named Simon, but as He reclined at the table (Jews had picked up the Roman custom of lying on couches while dining), a woman came in and, standing behind Him, began to weep. As her tears splashed on His feet she wiped them away with her hair, then kissed and anointed His feet with ointment. Simon said nothing, but decided that Jesus must not really be a prophet or He would have known that the woman was a sinner.

　　Jesus addressed what Simon was thinking. He pointed out that Simon had not shown Him the usual courtesy of providing a basin to wash His feet (a hospitable custom in that dusty climate), and didn't greet Him with an embrace or honor Him with anointing oil. The woman had done these things, because she was overflowing with love; she was filled with love because she knew the seriousness of her sins and the height of God's forgiveness. Simon was ignorant of his sin and his need, and as a result had little love. St. Andrew accuses himself of worse sins than the harlot's, and asks Jesus to "call him back" in repentance.

268.　**"Discolored Thine image . . . My beauty is destroyed."** We are made in the image and likeness of God, but our sins discolor and damage that beauty.

　　"My lamp is quenched." (Proverbs 20:27) "The spirit of man is the lamp of the LORD, searching all his innermost parts."

CHAPTER 30

267. I fall before Thee, and as tears I offer Thee my words. I have sinned as the harlot never sinned, and I have transgressed as no other man on earth. But take pity on Thy creature, O Master, and call me back.

Have mercy on me, O God, have mercy on me.

268. I have discolored Thine image and broken Thy commandment. All my beauty is destroyed and my lamp is quenched by the passions, O Savior. But take pity on me, as David sings, and "restore to me Thy joy."

Have mercy on me, O God, have mercy on me.

(Matthew 6:22-23) "The eye is the lamp of the body. So, if your eye is sound, your whole body will be full of light; but if your eye is not sound, your whole body will be full of darkness. If then the light in you is darkness, how great is the darkness!"

"Restore to me Thy joy." (Psalm 51:12) "Restore to me the joy of thy salvation, and uphold me with a willing spirit."

269. **"As David sings."** (Psalm 51:1) "Have mercy on me, O God, according to thy steadfast love; according to thy abundant mercy blot out my transgressions."

270. **"My days have vanished as the dream of one awakening."** (Psalm 39:4-5) "[L]et me know how fleeting my life is! Behold, thou hast made my days a few handbreadths, and my lifetime is as nothing in thy sight."

(Psalm 103:15-16) "As for man, his days are like grass; he flourishes like a flower of the field; for the wind passes over it, and it is gone, and its place knows it no more."

"Like Hezekiah." (2 Kings 20:1–6) King Hezekiah was ill, and the prophet Isaiah told him that he would not recover. (2 Kings 20:2-3) "Then Hezekiah turned his face to the wall, and prayed to the LORD . . . And Hezekiah wept bitterly." Isaiah then received word from the Lord that Hezekiah would recover.

CONSIDER

In the concluding verses of this canticle we call on our many strong friends for their prayers. We recall that St. Mary of Egypt prayed to the Theotokos and was given strength to overcome her fierce passions; that she loved Christ, and He bestowed on her repentance. We ask St. Mary and St. Andrew to pray for us; we glorify the Trinity and the Virgin Theotokos.

Every person is nagged by a sense of having a black hole inside. At the very center of our being, far from the seamless exterior that our friends can see, far beneath the cloudy depths that we conceal but can partly understand, there are blank measureless regions we can't comprehend at all. At these depths, we feel utterly alone. But underneath the furthest depths of incomprehensible darkness, a bit of light begins to emerge. It is the light of Christ, who made us, and as Creator has a fundamental place and power beneath any region of our awareness. And in the farther light, we find we are not alone. We have friends, eternal friends like St.

130

269. Turn back, repent, uncover all that thou hast hidden. Say unto God, to whom all things are known: Thou alone knowest my secrets, O Savior; "Have mercy on me," as David sings, "according to Thy mercy."

Have mercy on me, O God, have mercy on me.

270. My days have vanished as the dream of one awaking: And so, like Hezekiah, I weep upon my bed, that years may be added to my life. But what Isaiah will come to thee, my soul, except the God of all?

Have mercy on me, O God, have mercy on me.

271. Raising thy cry to the pure Mother of God, thou hast driven back the fury of the passions that violently assailed thee, and put to shame the enemy who sought to make thee stumble. But give thy help in trouble now to me also, thy servant.

Have mercy on me, O God, have mercy on me.

272. He whom thou hast loved, O Mother, whom thou hast desired, in whose footsteps thou hast followed: He it was who found thee and gave thee repentance, for He is God compassionate. Pray to Him without ceasing, that we may be delivered from passions and distress.

Holy Father Andrew, pray to God for us.

273. Set me firmly on the rock of faith, O father, through thine intercessions; fence me round with fear of God, O Andrew; grant repentance to me now, I beseech thee,

Mary and St. Andrew, who are one with us in the body of Christ—not a motionless order of beings like marble statues, but a living unity in Life Himself.

Think about these powerful and loving friends, who are no longer bound by time. What will you ask them to pray for?

and deliver me from the snare of the enemies that seek my life.

Glory to the Father, and to the Son, and to the Holy Spirit.

274. O simple and undivided Trinity, one consubstantial Nature: Thou art praised as Light and Lights, one Holy and three Holies. Sing, O my soul, and glorify life and lives, the God of all.

Both now and ever and unto ages of ages. Amen.

275. We praise thee, we bless thee, we venerate thee, O Mother of God: for thou hast given birth to One of the undivided Trinity, thy Son and God, and thou hast opened the heavenly places to us on earth.

276. We have sinned, we have transgressed, we have done evil in Thy sight; we have not kept or followed Thy commandments. But reject us not utterly, O God of our fathers.

CHAPTER 31

EXPLORE

278.   "Coals of immaterial fire." Just as Jesus was transfigured with uncreated light on Mt. Tabor, the apostles have become bearers of "immaterial fire." This is our goal as well, to be cleansed through repentance to the point that we can also bear His fire.

279.   "Caused the ill-founded walls of the enemy to fall." The preaching of the apostles is likened to Joshua's trumpets, which made the walls of Jericho fall (Joshua 6:20).

280.   "Break in pieces the idols." Ezekiel prophesied to Israel that its idols and temples of foreign gods would be destroyed. "[Y]our high places [shall be] ruined, so that your altars will be waste and ruined, your idols broken and destroyed, your incense altars cut down, and your works wiped out" (Ezekiel 6:6).

"Consecrated temples." We are being built into a temple with the apostles. (Ephesians 2:19–21) "[Y]ou are fellow citizens with the saints and members of the household of God, built upon the foundation of the apostles and prophets, Christ Jesus himself being the cornerstone, in whom the whole structure is joined together and grows into a holy temple in the Lord."

281.   St. Andrew sets forth paradoxes about the Virgin Theotokos: The Creator of all, who fills and exceeds everything that is, was contained within her body. The God who is "upholding the universe by his word of power" (Hebrews 1:3) was held in her arms. The One who feeds and sustains all Creation was a baby fed at her breast.

CHAPTER 31

277. The eternal King of glory, before whom the powers of heaven tremble and the ranks of angels stand in fear, O ye priests praise and ye people exalt above all for ever.

Apostles of Christ, pray to God for us.

278. As coals of immaterial fire, O apostles, burn up my material passions and kindle within me now a longing for divine love.

Apostles of Christ, pray to God for us.

279. Let us honor the well-tuned trumpets of the Word, which have caused the ill-founded walls of the enemy to fall, and have firmly established the ramparts of the knowledge of God.

Apostles of Christ, pray to God for us.

280. Break in pieces the passionate idols of my soul, as ye broke in pieces the temples and pillars of the enemy, O apostles of the Lord, consecrated temples.

Most holy Theotokos, save us.

281. O pure Virgin, thou hast contained Him who by nature cannot be contained; thou hast held Him who upholds all things; thou hast given suck to Him who sustains the creation, Christ the Giver of Life.

283. **"O apostles . . . have built the whole Church."** (Matthew 16:18) "You are Peter, and on this rock I will build my church, and the powers of death shall not prevail against it." Peter and the other apostles are the "foundation" (Ephesians 2:19-20) upon which the "holy temple," the Church, the body of Christ, is built.

284. **"Sounding the trumpets of the dogmas."** The truth of the gospel overthrows idolatry, as the walls of Jericho fell at the sound of trumpets.

CONSIDER

As the three young men sang in the fiery furnace, King Nebuchadnezzer was astonished and looked in. (Daniel 3:24-25) "Did we not cast three men bound into the fire?" he asked his counselors. "But I see four men loose, walking in the midst of the fire, and they are not hurt; and the appearance of the fourth is like a son of the gods."

In 1916, Sir Ernest Shackleton organized an expedition to Antarctica which quickly succumbed to catastrophe. His ship, the Endurance, was locked in ice, then crushed and sank. His new goal was simply to get all his men back to England safely. It seemed impossible, and yet he succeeded.

After seventeen months of excruciating conditions, Shackleton and two other crewmen set out to reach a whaling station on the far side of South Georgia Island. The interior of the island had never been charted and whalers considered it impassable. The three would have to climb windswept peaks and descend steep precipices, and cross ice fields that concealed deadly crevasses. They could never stop to rest: rest meant sleep, and sleep meant death.

Shackleton wrote later, "During that long and racking march of thirty-six hours over the unnamed mountains and glaciers of South Georgia, it seemed to me often that we were four, not three. I said nothing to my companions, but afterwards Worsley said to me, 'Boss, I had a curious feeling that there was another person with us.'"

We sometimes hear of tragedies that seem unbearable, and as we picture someone's last hours we may feel overwhelmed with helpless grief. But we don't really know what it was like. It may be that, in the last moments, the person discovered he was not

136

282. The eternal King of glory, before whom the powers of heaven tremble and the ranks of angels stand in fear, O ye priests praise and ye people exalt above all for ever.

Apostles of Christ, pray to God for us.

283. O apostles of Christ, with the Spirit as architect ye have built the whole Church, and within it ye bless Christ for ever.

Apostles of Christ, pray to God for us.

284. Sounding the trumpets of the dogmas, the apostles have overthrown all the error of idolatry, exalting Christ above all for ever.

Apostles of Christ, pray to God for us.

285. O noble company of the apostles who watch over the world and dwell in heaven, deliver from danger those who ever sing your praises.

Glory to the Father, and to the Son, and to the Holy Spirit.

286. O threefold Sun, all-radiant Sovereignty of God, O Nature one in glory, one in throne: Father all-creating, Son, and Spirit of God, I praise Thee for ever.

Both now and ever and unto ages of ages. Amen.

287. As a throne honored and most high, let us praise in ceaseless song the Mother of God, O ye peoples, for she alone is both a Mother and a Virgin after childbirth.

alone. Perhaps wherever he was, in the hands of a powerful torturer, or lost in cruel and icy mountains, he suddenly saw another person with him—an unknown Friend whom he had, somehow, always known—one whose appearance was "like a son of the gods."

COMMENTARY
CHAPTER 32

EXPLORE

288. **"Before Him tremble cherubim and seraphim."** Another *irmos* taken from the Song of the Three Young Men.

Cherubim (singular, cherub) are mentioned throughout the Scriptures. They represent the throne of God. (Psalm 99:1) "The LORD reigns; let the peoples tremble! He sits enthroned upon the cherubim; let the earth quake!"

Seraphim (singular, seraph), a type of six-winged angel, are mentioned only once in Scripture. In Isaiah's vision, he saw the Lord's majestic presence filling the temple, as seraphim flew before him crying "Holy, holy, holy" (Isaiah 6:1–4). The foundation of the temple was shaken at the voice of the angel.

290. **"Riding in the chariot."** As his disciple Elisha watched, the prophet Elijah was carried to heaven in a chariot of fire. (2 Kings 2:11) "And as they still went on and talked, behold, a chariot of fire and horses of fire separated the two of them. And Elijah went up by a whirlwind into heaven."

291. **"With the mantle of Elijah."** (2 Kings 2:13-14) After the chariot took Elijah up, Elisha "took the mantle of Elijah that had fallen from him, and went back and stood on the bank of the Jordan. Then he took the mantle of Elijah that had fallen from him, and struck the water, saying, 'Where is the LORD, the God of Elijah?' And when he had struck the water, the water was parted to the one side and to the other; and Elisha went over."

CHAPTER 32

288. The hosts of heaven give Him glory; before Him tremble cherubim and seraphim; let everything that has breath and all creation praise Him, bless Him, and exalt Him above all for ever.

Have mercy on me, O God, have mercy on me.

289. I have sinned, O Savior, have mercy on me. Awaken my mind and turn me back; accept me in repentance and take pity on me as I cry: against Thee only have I sinned; I have done evil, have mercy on me.

Have mercy on me, O God, have mercy on me.

290. Riding in the chariot of the virtues, Elijah was lifted up to heaven, high above earthly things. Reflect, my soul, on his ascent.

Have mercy on me, O God, have mercy on me.

291. With the mantle of Elijah, Elisha made the stream of Jordan stand still on either side: but in this grace, my soul, thou hast no share, by reason of thy greed and uncontrolled desires.

Have mercy on me, O God, have mercy on me.

292. **"Double portion."** (2 Kings 2:10) Elisha asked Elijah that he would be able to receive "a double share of your spirit." Elijah replied, "You have asked a hard thing; yet, if you see me as I am being taken from you, it shall be so for you; but if you do not see me, it shall not be so." Elisha did see Elijah when he was taken up.

293. **"The Shunammite woman."** (2 Kings 4:8–10) This wealthy woman gave hospitality to the prophet Elisha, and when she saw that he passed her way regularly, she built and furnished a room for his use.

    "Cast out weeping from the bridal chamber." (Matthew 22:12-13) The king said to the uninvited guest, "'Friend, how did you get in here without a wedding garment?' And he was speechless. Then the king said to the attendants, 'Bind him hand and foot, and cast him into the outer darkness; there men will weep and gnash their teeth.'"

294. **"Polluted thoughts of Gehazi."** (2 Kings 5:1–27) Naaman was a commander of the Syrian army, and was a leper. He was healed by the prophet Elisha, and offered him a gift, but Elisha refused to take one. Elisha's servant Gehazi, however, overheard this conversation. He ran after Naaman and said that his master now had need of money and expensive garments, which Naaman was glad to give. But when Gehazi returned home, Elisha said, "Did I not go with you in spirit when the man turned from his chariot to meet you? Was it a time to accept money and garments, olive orchards and vineyards, sheep and oxen, menservants and maidservants? Therefore the leprosy of Naaman shall cleave to you, and to your descendants for ever."

295. **"Thou hast followed Uzziah."** (2 Chronicles 26:16–21) King Uzziah took it on himself to offer incense in the house of the Lord, something permitted only to priests. The chief priest Azariah pleaded with him not to do this. "Then Uzziah was angry. Now he had a censer in his hand to burn incense, and when he became angry with the priests leprosy broke out on his forehead."

296. **"Men of Nineveh repented."** (Jonah 3:1–10) The prophet Jonah was sent by God to preach a warning to the city of Nineveh, even though it was a foreign land not occupied by the Israelites. Jonah refused and was attempting to escape by ship when a storm arose, and he was tossed overboard and swallowed by a great fish. When the fish spit him out on dry land, at last Jonah made the journey to Nineveh. The people did repent, from the king to the lowliest, throughout the city.

292. Elisha once took up the mantle of Elijah, and received a double portion of grace from the Lord: but in this grace, my soul, thou hast no share, by reason of thy greed and uncontrolled desires.

Have mercy on me, O God, have mercy on me.

293. The Shunammite woman gladly entertained the righteous prophet: but in thy house, my soul, thou hast not welcomed stranger or traveler; and so thou shalt be cast out weeping from the bridal chamber.

Have mercy on me, O God, have mercy on me.

294. O wretched soul, always thou hast imitated the polluted thoughts of Gehazi. Cast from thee, at least in thine old age, his love of money. Flee from the fire of hell, turn away from thy wickedness.

Have mercy on me, O God, have mercy on me.

295. Thou hast followed Uzziah, my soul, and hast his leprosy in double form; for thy thoughts are wicked, and thine acts unlawful. Leave what thou hast, and hasten to repentance.

Have mercy on me, O God, have mercy on me.

296. O my soul, thou hast heard how the men of Nineveh repented before God in sackcloth and ashes. Yet thou hast not followed them, but art more wicked than all who sinned before the Law and after.

Have mercy on me, O God, have mercy on me.

297. **"Jeremiah in the muddy pit."** (Jeremiah 38:6) The prophet Jeremiah had been preaching to the citizens of Jerusalem that the army of Babylon would conquer the city, a message that was demoralizing the soldiers. The king permitted his princes to get Jeremiah out of the way: "So they took Jeremiah and cast him into the cistern of Malchiah, the king's son, which was in the court of the guard, letting Jeremiah down by ropes. And there was no water in the cistern, but only mire, and Jeremiah sank in the mire."

"And asked to be given tears." (Jeremiah 9:1) "O that my head were waters, and my eyes a fountain of tears, that I might weep day and night for the slain of the daughter of my people!"

CONSIDER

Naaman, Gehazi, and Uzziah were all afflicted with leprosy; Naaman was cured of it miraculously, and the other two received it suddenly, as a result of their sins. This leprosy seems almost like evidence of their sins, as if Gehazi's greed and Uzziah's angry pride burst out visibly for all to see. It is like Pinocchio's wooden nose, which grew longer as he spoke lies.

Few sins are visible to onlookers. What sinful thoughts or behaviors would become apparent to those around you, if God wrote them visibly on your skin, as happened to Gehazi and Uzziah? It may not be enough of a spur to repentance, to consider the possibility of eventual punishment, or present alienation from God. But if your sins would suddenly be indelible and obvious to all, would you change? Which sins?

COMMENTARY
CHAPTER 33

EXPLORE

298. **"Jonah fled to Tarshish."** When God commanded his prophet Jonah to go preach repentance to the people of Nineveh, a city far inland to the northeast, Jonah immediately hopped on a ship headed west. Nineveh was the capital of the Assyrian empire, and was widely hated throughout the Middle East. While a Hebrew prophet might find it an appealing thought that God might punish the Ninevites, it was not so appealing that they might heed the warning and repent. Jonah, aware of **"the loving-kindness of God,"** preferred that his prophecy of destruction come true.

297. Thou hast heard, my soul, how Jeremiah in the muddy pit cried out with lamentations for the city of Zion and asked to be given tears. Follow his life of lamentation and be saved.

Have mercy on me, O God, have mercy on me.

CHAPTER 33

298. Jonah fled to Tarshish, foreseeing the conversion of the men of Nineveh; for as a prophet he knew the loving-kindness of God, but he was jealous that his prophecy should not be proved false.

Have mercy on me, O God, have mercy on me.

299. "Daniel stopped the mouths of the wild beasts." (Daniel 6:14–22) The governors of Babylon were jealous of Daniel, who had risen in the esteem of King Darius. They persuaded the king to sign a decree that no one must pray to anyone but him, then pointed out that Daniel was breaking the decree. "Then the king, when he heard these words, was much distressed, and set his mind to deliver Daniel; and he labored till the sun went down to rescue him." In the end, the king was forced to deliver Daniel to the appointed punishment, sealing him in a lions' den. "The king said to Daniel, 'May your God, whom you serve continually, deliver you!'" The king spent the night in fasting, and the next day Daniel came out of the den unharmed.

"The Children with Azarias." (Daniel 3:23) The three young men thrown into the "burning fiery furnace" are sometimes referred to as "the three children."

300. "All the names of the Old Testament." St. Andrew has completed an astonishingly thorough overview of the Old Testament, given the research tools of his time. The cycle of worship he participated in with his brother monks would have brought the Scriptures to his ears continually.

302. "Like the thief I cry to Thee, 'Remember me.'" (Luke 23:42) The thief on the cross next to Jesus said, "Jesus, remember me when you come into your kingdom."

"Like Peter I weep bitterly." (Matthew 26:75) After Peter had denied Jesus three times, the Lord turned and looked at him. "And Peter remembered the saying of Jesus, 'Before the cock crows, you will deny me three times.' And he went out and wept bitterly." Only Peter would have known about this; we know the story because he told it on himself.

"Like the publican I call out, 'Forgive me, Savior.'" (Luke 18:13) "But the tax collector, standing far off, would not even lift up his eyes to heaven, but beat his breast, saying, 'God, be merciful to me a sinner!'"

"Like the harlot I shed tears." (Luke 7:37-38) "[A] woman of the city, who was a sinner . . . brought an alabaster flask of ointment, and standing behind him at his feet, weeping, she began to wet his feet with her tears, and wiped them with the hair of her head."

"Entreaties of the woman of Canaan." A Canaanite woman begged Jesus to heal her daughter, who was possessed.

299. My soul, thou hast heard how Daniel stopped the mouths of the wild beasts in the lions' den; and thou knowest how the Children with Azarias quenched through their faith the flames of the fiery furnace.

Have mercy on me, O God, have mercy on me.

300. All the names of the Old Testament have I set before thee, my soul, as an example. Imitate the holy acts of the righteous and flee from the sins of the wicked.

Have mercy on me, O God, have mercy on me.

301. O righteous Judge and Savior, have mercy on me and deliver me from the fire that threatens me, and from the punishment that I deserve to suffer at the judgment. Before the end comes, grant me remission through virtue and repentance.

Have mercy on me, O God, have mercy on me.

302. Like the thief I cry to Thee, "Remember me;" like Peter I weep bitterly; like the publican I call out, "Forgive me, Savior;" like the harlot I shed tears. Accept my lamentation, as once Thou hast accepted the entreaties of the woman of Canaan.

Have mercy on me, O God, have mercy on me.

(Matthew 15:22) "[A] Canaanite woman from that region came out and cried, 'Have mercy on me, O Lord, Son of David.'"

303. **"Pour in oil and wine."** When the good Samaritan found the beaten man he "went to him and bound up his wounds, pouring on oil and wine" (Luke 10:34).

304. **"Like the woman with an issue of blood."** (Luke 8:43-44) "And a woman who had had a flow of blood for twelve years and could not be healed by any one, came up behind him, and touched the fringe of his garment; and immediately her flow of blood ceased."

305. **"I weep as Martha and Mary wept for Lazarus."** (John 11:1–44) Lazarus and his sisters Mary and Martha lived in Bethany, and were good friends of Jesus. When Lazarus died, Jesus went to Bethany and found the sisters grieving for their brother, then wept himself, before raising Lazarus from the dead.

"The alabaster box of my tears." (Mark 14:3) "[A] woman came with an alabaster jar of ointment of pure nard, very costly, and she broke the jar and poured it over his head." (This is a different incident from the earlier one, in which the harlot wept over Jesus' feet.)

"Like the harlot I cry out." (Luke 7:37-38) The harlot wept continuously.

CONSIDER

As the Canon approaches its conclusion, St. Andrew brings together all the Scriptures he has been contemplating in a symphony. It is hard to repent, because we find it hard to trust God to be merciful; because we shield ourselves from recognizing our own sinfulness; and because the murky realm of our sins is something we don't even understand very well. But St. Andrew holds up as examples multitudes who have gone before us, in order to show us what heartfelt repentance looks like and how God responds to it.

Peter betrayed Christ; when servants of the high priest questioned him casually around the courtyard fire, he backed away in confusion, swearing by an oath and invoking a curse on himself, "I do not know the man!" (Matthew 26:72, 74).

Judas also betrayed Christ. When he realized that Jesus had been hauled off for execution, he was stricken. He went back to the temple and tried to return the money he'd received. He told the priests, "'I have sinned in betraying innocent blood'. . . . And

303. O Savior, heal the putrefaction of my humbled soul, for Thou art the one Physician; apply plaster, and pour in oil and wine—works of repentance, and compunction with tears.

Have mercy on me, O God, have mercy on me.

304. Like the woman of Canaan, I cry to Thee, "Have mercy on me, Son of David." Like the woman with an issue of blood, I touch the hem of Thy garment. I weep as Martha and Mary wept for Lazarus.

Have mercy on me, O God, have mercy on me.

305. As precious ointment, O Savior, I empty on Thine head the alabaster box of my tears. Like the harlot, I cry out to Thee, seeking mercy: I bring my prayer and ask to receive forgiveness.

Have mercy on me, O God, have mercy on me.

throwing down the pieces of silver in the temple, he departed; and he went and hanged himself" (Matthew 27:4-5).

Both apostles, who sat at Jesus' feet and listened to Him every day, who received the bread and wine from Jesus' own hands at the Last Supper, betrayed Him mere hours later. But one of them repented. Peter "wept bitterly" and returned to Christ, and now is a pillar in the house of God. Judas was consumed with bitterness, self-reproaches, and misery, and cast himself into Hades. The kind of despair that causes a person to give up on God is a particular kind of deadly sin, often translated (misleadingly) "sloth." It's not laziness that's the problem, but the conclusion that no matter what you do it will make no difference, so why try? Healthy repentance, on the other hand, ends in hope.

The lesson of Judas and St. Peter is that the nature of the sin does not matter. Any sin can be forgiven. The only thing preventing salvation is a person's willingness to repent and come back to God in humility. Don't be afraid to bring God your very "worst" sins; you probably don't even know yet what your worst sin is. God knows, and already forgives; it is up to you to come for reconciliation.

COMMENTARY
CHAPTER 34

EXPLORE

306. **"Against Thee alone have I sinned."** (Psalm 51:4a) "Against thee, thee only, have I sinned, and done that which is evil in thy sight."

307. **"As a shepherd seek the lost sheep."** (Psalm 119:176) "I have gone astray like a lost sheep; seek thy servant, for I do not forget thy commandments."

(Luke 15:4-5) "What man of you, having a hundred sheep, if he has lost one of them, does not leave the ninety-nine in the wilderness, and go after the one which is lost, until he finds it? And when he has found it, he lays it on his shoulders, rejoicing."

(John 10:11) "I am the good shepherd. The good shepherd lays down his life for the sheep."

308. **"When Thou sittest upon Thy throne."** (Daniel 7:9-10) "As I looked, thrones were placed and one that was ancient of days took his seat; his raiment was white as snow, and the hair of his head like pure wool; his throne was fiery flames, its wheels were

CHAPTER 34

306. No one has sinned against Thee as I have; yet accept even me, compassionate Savior, for I repent in fear and cry with longing: Against Thee alone have I sinned; I have transgressed, have mercy on me.

Have mercy on me, O God, have mercy on me.

307. Spare the work of Thine own hands, O Savior, and as Shepherd seek the lost sheep that has gone astray. Snatch me from the wolf and make me a nursling in the pasture of Thine own flock.

Have mercy on me, O God, have mercy on me.

308. When Thou sittest upon Thy throne, O merciful Judge, and revealest Thy dread glory, O Christ, what fear there will be then! When the furnace burns with fire, and all shrink back in terror before Thy judgment seat.

Have mercy on me, O God, have mercy on me.

309. The Mother of the Light that never sets illumined thee and freed thee from the darkness of thy passions. O Mary, who hast received the grace of the Spirit, give light to those who praise thee with faith.

Have mercy on me, O God, have mercy on me.

burning fire. A stream of fire issued and came forth from before him; a thousand thousands served him, and ten thousand times ten thousand stood before him; the court sat in judgment, and the books were opened."

(Matthew 24:30) "[T]hen will appear the sign of the Son of man in heaven, and then all the tribes of the earth will mourn, and they will see the Son of man coming on the clouds of heaven with power and great glory."

(Matthew 25:31) "When the Son of man comes in his glory, and all the angels with him, then he will sit on his glorious throne."

CONSIDER

At the end of time, when the sky will vanish "like a scroll that is rolled up" (Revelation 6:14), one who is "ancient of days" will take His seat for judgment. It is not God the Father, but the Son, Jesus Christ. "The Father judges no one, but has given all judgment to the Son" (John 5:22).

St. John described the appearance of Christ in his Revelation: "[I]n the midst of the lampstands [was] one like a Son of man, clothed with a long robe and with a golden girdle round his breast; his head and his hair were white as white wool, white as snow; his eyes were like a flame of fire, his feet were like burnished bronze, refined as in a furnace, and his voice was like the sound of many waters . . . his face was like the sun shining in full strength" (Revelation 1:13–16).

On that day we will not be facing an unknown, faceless judge who has stern, by-the-book convictions. We will be facing our Friend. His hands still bear the wounds of the nails, and His voice is the same one that has been calling us all our lives. As He sorts between sheep and goats, it won't be hard for Him to tell which is which. A lifetime turns you into one or the other. It will be too late then to repent of all the goatish decades, which passed so gently, imperceptibly, one lazy day after another. At the end of a lifetime of living like a goat, it will be too late to turn into a humble, trusting lamb. Today is the day of salvation.

(Psalm 95:6-7) "O come, let us worship and bow down, let us kneel before the LORD, our Maker! For he is our God, and we are the people of his pasture, and the sheep of his hand. O that today you would hearken to his voice!"

310. The holy Zosimas was struck with amazement, O Mother, beholding in thee a wonder truly strange and new. For he saw an angel in the body and was filled with astonishment, praising Christ unto all ages.

Have mercy on me, O God, have mercy on me.

311. Since thou hast boldness before the Lord, O Andrew, honored renown of Crete, I beseech thee, intercede that I may find deliverance from the bonds of iniquity through thy prayers, O teacher, glory of holy monks.

COMMENTARY
CHAPTER 35

EXPLORE

313. **"As from purple silk."** In the ancient world, the most expensive and precious fabric dye was a crimson-purple derived from shellfish. Due to its rarity it became an emblem of royalty. The **"spiritual robe of Emmanuel"** ("Emmanuel" means "God with us," Matthew 1:23), the flesh of the Lord Jesus, was woven in the womb of the Virgin Theotokos.

314. **"Let everything that has breath and all creation praise Him."** (Psalm 148:1-2) "Praise the LORD! Praise the LORD from the heavens, praise him in the heights! Praise him, all his angels, praise him, all his host!"

   (Psalm 150:6) "Let everything that breathes praise the LORD! Praise the LORD!"

315. Luke 1:46–55 is the Virgin Mary's song of praise. At the time she was pregnant with our Lord, and had gone to visit her cousin Elizabeth, who was six month's pregnant with St. John the Forerunner. When Mary stepped into Elizabeth's house and greeted her, Elizabeth felt her son leap in her womb.

   Elizabeth exclaimed, "Blessed are you among women, and blessed is the fruit of your womb! And why is this granted me, that the mother of my Lord should come to me? For behold, when the voice of your greeting came to my ears, the babe in my womb leaped for joy. And blessed is she who believed that there would be a fulfillment of what was spoken to her from the Lord" (Luke 1:42–45). Mary responded with the words of this hymn of praise.

152

CHAPTER 35

We bless the Lord, Father, Son, and Holy Spirit.

312. Father without beginning, coeternal Son, and loving Comforter, the Spirit of righteousness, Begetter of the Word of God, Word of the Eternal Father, Spirit living and creative: O Trinity in Unity, have mercy on me.

Both now and ever and unto ages of ages. Amen.

313. As from purple silk, O undefiled Virgin, the spiritual robe of Emmanuel, His flesh, was woven in thy womb. Therefore we honor thee as Theotokos in very truth.

We praise, bless, and worship the Lord,
magnifying Him unto all ages.

314. The hosts of heaven give Him glory; before Him tremble cherubim and seraphim; let everything that has breath and all creation praise Him, bless Him, and exalt Him above all for ever.

THE CANTICLE OF THE THEOTOKOS

315. My soul magnifies the Lord, and my spirit rejoices in God my Savior, For He has regarded the low estate of His handmaiden.

316. **"All generations will call me blessed."** Christians throughout the centuries have recognized the blessing God bestowed on Mary, and the **"great things"** He did for her.

317. **"His mercy is on those who fear Him."** This fear is not terror, but reverent awe. We come to God in utter honesty about ourselves, in humility and repentance, and discover that His mercy is pouring forth to meet us, surrounding and healing us. This encounter with His mercy, so abundant and so undeserved, astounds and humbles us. We are able then to be even more honest about ourselves, to face deeper truths that we could not admit before, and return to Him in even greater reverence and awe.

318. The Virgin Theotokos is more honorable and glorious than the angels because of her role in the Incarnation. The cherubim were the throne of God, but her body contained the Creator of all. The popular Lutheran hymn, "Ye Watchers and Ye Holy Ones," attributes similar honor to the Virgin as it envisions her singing praise to God in heaven:

"O higher than the cherubim, More glorious than the seraphim,

Lead their praises, Alleluia!

Thou Bearer of the eternal Word, Most gracious, magnify the Lord,

Alleluia! Alleluia!"

(John A. L. Riley, 1906; inspired by Psalm 148)

CONSIDER

The Virgin Theotokos was not part of the public preaching of the early church, yet it seems that she was treated with great affection within the community of faith from the beginning. A book called the *Protoevangelion of James* recounts her conception, birth, childhood, and marriage to St. Joseph in colorful and loving detail. We might presume such a book would be a work of medieval imagination—but it was written about the year 150 AD. Beliefs about the Virgin were so uncontroversial that they didn't come up for debate in that argumentative age, except when they had to do with the divinity of Christ. (Some proposed that when Jesus was in Mary's womb He was not yet God).

The main thing to catch about early Christian feeling for the Virgin Theotokos is affection. Early Christians loved her. They

154

316. For behold, henceforth all generations will call me blessed;
For He who is mighty has done great things for me, and holy is His name.

317. And His mercy is on those who fear Him from generation to generation.

318. He has shown strength with His arm, He has scattered the proud in the imagination of their hearts,

319. He has put down the mighty from their thrones, and exalted those of low degree;

320. He has filled the hungry with good things, and the rich He has sent empty away.

321. He has helped His servant Israel, in remembrance of His mercy, as He spoke to our fathers, to Abraham, and to his posterity for ever.

322. More honorable than the cherubim, and more glorious beyond compare than the seraphim, thou who without corruption barest God the Word, and art truly Theotokos, we magnify thee.

felt she was their mother, too, and with good reason: Jesus said so. (John 19:26-27) "When Jesus saw his mother, and the disciple whom he loved standing near, he said to his mother, 'Woman, behold, your son!' Then he said to the disciple, 'Behold, your mother!'" John took Mary to his own home and cared for her till the end of her life—another indication that she had no other sons but Jesus.

Sometimes we make friends with somebody, and then later get to meet his family, and find out that we enjoy his parents and siblings just as much. When we meet Jesus, we get Mary "in the bargain." She is not dead, but living in the presence of God, ready to befriend us, ready to intercede for us. Follow in the footsteps of the early Christians and begin to bring your confidences, fears, and needs to this powerful prayer partner and friend. "Behold, your mother!"

COMMENTARY
CHAPTER 36

EXPLORE

323. **"Saved through thee."** Only Christ saves us, of course; this is a shorthand way of thanking the Virgin for her prayers, which sustain us as we continue in the path of salvation.

324. **"Fountains of the water of salvation."** (Proverbs 18:4) "The words of a man's mouth are deep waters; the fountain of wisdom is a gushing stream."

325. **"Deep waters . . . Save me as Thou hast saved Peter."** (Matthew 14:29–31) "So Peter got out of the boat and walked on the water and came to Jesus; but when he saw the wind, he was afraid, and beginning to sink he cried out, 'Lord, save me.' Jesus immediately reached out his hand and caught him, saying to him, 'O man of little faith, why did you doubt?'"

326. **"Salt that gives savor."** (Matthew 5:13) "You are the salt of the earth; but if salt has lost its taste, how shall its saltness be restored?"

   "Dry up the rottenness." Salt was used in the ancient world not only as a flavoring but as a preservative.

327. **"Grant me the spirit of mourning."** (Matthew 5:4) "Blessed are those who mourn, for they shall be comforted."

CHAPTER 36

323. Saved through thee, pure Virgin, we confess thee to be truly Theotokos, and with the choirs of angels we magnify thee.

Apostles of Christ, pray to God for us.

324. Ye were revealed, O apostles, as fountains of the water of salvation: bring refreshment to my soul that faints from the thirst of sin.

Apostles of Christ, pray to God for us.

325. I am swimming in the deep waters of destruction and have come near to drowning: with Thy right hand, O Lord, save me as Thou hast saved Peter.

Apostles of Christ, pray to God for us.

326. Ye are the salt that gives savor to the teachings of salvation: dry up the rottenness of my mind and dispel the darkness of my ignorance.

Most Holy Theotokos, save us.

327. O Lady, thou hast brought forth our Joy: Grant me the spirit of mourning that in the coming Day of Judgment I may be comforted by God.

329. **"Intercessor."** The Virgin Mary is an intercessor in the sense that anyone would be who intercedes for another person.

"In thee, O Virgin, the fullness of the Godhead came to dwell bodily." (Colossians 2:9) Because Christ was in her womb, and "in [Christ] the whole fullness of deity dwells bodily."

331. **"Catching rational fish."** (Mark 1:17) "Jesus said to them, 'Follow me and I will make you become fishers of men.'"

Converts to Christ, those "fish" caught by the apostles, are "rational" in the sense that the dark confusion of the evil one has been driven away and their minds have been illuminated. It does not mean "rational" in the sense of being dryly logical.

332. **"Delivered from temptation."** (Luke 22:46) "Rise and pray that you may not enter into temptation."

(Matthew 6:13) "And lead us not into temptation, But deliver us from evil."

CONSIDER

This familiar line from the Lord's Prayer can be perplexing. Why would God lead us into temptation? That would seem to give us an excuse when we give in to sin, if God had laid a tempting trap. St. James demolishes this idea: "Let no one say when he is tempted, 'I am tempted by God;' for God cannot be tempted with evil and he himself tempts no one; but each person is tempted when he is lured and enticed by his own desire" (James 1:13-14).

The key is to see this line as being a duplication of the same thought, as happens commonly in Hebrew poetry. (Look up Psalm 1 for an example of this; every idea is stated two or three times). "Lead us not into temptation" is restated in the next phrase, "But deliver us from evil." In fact, the Greek reads, "deliver us from the evil," that is, the personification of evil, the evil one. As we follow God as our shepherd and guide, we trust Him to keep us safe from paths that would expose us to the temptation and power of the evil one.

Yet St. James reminds us that we can't blame the evil one for our falls. "Each person is tempted . . . by his own desire." Nobody can say, "The devil made me do it!" The devil can lay traps, but we are responsible for stepping into them. St. Paul says, "God is faithful, and he will not let you be tempted beyond

158

328. Saved through thee, pure Virgin, we confess thee to be truly Theotokos, and with the choirs of angels we magnify thee.

329. With all generations we magnify thee, intercessor between heaven and earth. For in thee, O Virgin, the fullness of the Godhead came to dwell bodily.

Apostles of Christ, pray to God for us.

330. We magnify you in our hymns, O glorious company of the apostles: for ye have been revealed as shining lights of the inhabited earth, driving out error.

Apostles of Christ, pray to God for us.

331. O blessed apostles, catching rational fish with the net of the gospel, bring them always as an offering to Christ.

Apostles of Christ, pray to God for us.

332. In your prayers to God remember us, we entreat you, O apostles. May we be delivered from all temptation, for lovingly we sing your praises.

Glory to the Father, and to the Son, and to the Holy Spirit.

333. I sing Thy praises, Unity in three Persons, Father, Son, and Spirit, one God, consubstantial Trinity, equal in power and without beginning.

Both now and ever and unto ages of ages. Amen.

your strength, but with the temptation will also provide the way of escape, that you may be able to endure it" (1 Corinthians 10:13).

There's no guarantee that the "way of escape" will be easy; it may be a narrow escape indeed. "Enter by the narrow gate; for the gate is wide and the way is easy, that leads to destruction, and those who enter by it are many. For the gate is narrow and the way is hard, that leads to life, and those who find it are few." (Matthew 7:13-14). We can ask God to keep us from paths of temptation, but in the end, it is our responsibility where we choose to go.

COMMENTARY
CHAPTER 37

EXPLORE

336. **"All generations magnify thee."** The *irmos* of Canticle Nine recalls the Virgin's words in the ninth biblical canticle, "All generations will call me blessed."

337.   As we draw near the end of the Canon, St. Andrew's words toll like a bell. He recognizes that his body is exhausted and his earthly life is at an end.

   "When the Judge comes to examine thy deeds." (1 Peter 1:17) "And if you invoke as Father him who judges each one impartially according to his deeds, conduct yourselves with fear throughout the time of your exile."

338.   **"Thou, my soul, hast followed the second of these, not the first."** St. Andrew compels himself to recognize his failure to follow the example of the righteous throughout Scripture.

334. With all generations we call thee blessed, O Mother and Virgin: through thee we are delivered from the curse, for thou hast borne the Lord our Joy.

335. With all generations we magnify thee, intercessor between heaven and earth. For in thee, O Virgin, the fullness of the Godhead came to dwell bodily.

CHAPTER 37

336. Conception without seed; nativity past understanding, from a Mother who never knew a man; childbearing undefiled. For the birth of God makes both natures new. Therefore, as Bride and Mother of God, with true worship all generations magnify thee.

Have mercy on me, O God, have mercy on me.

337. My mind is wounded, my body has grown feeble, my spirit is sick, my speech has lost its power, my life is dead; the end is at the door. What shalt thou do, then, miserable soul, when the Judge comes to examine thy deeds?

Have mercy on me, O God, have mercy on me.

338. I have put before thee, my soul, Moses' account of the creation of the world, and after that all the recognized Scriptures that tell thee the story of the righteous and the

339. "The Law is powerless." The solemnity of these verses reaches a crescendo. The whole of the Scripture has no capacity to turn a heart that prefers self-willed hardness.

341. "He performed all that belongs to my nature, only without sin." (Hebrews 4:15) "For we have not a high priest who is unable to sympathize with our weaknesses, but one who in every respect has been tempted as we are, yet without sinning."

342. "Pharisees and publicans and adulterers pass through it before thee." (Matthew 21:31) "Truly, I say to you, the tax collectors and the harlots go into the kingdom of God before you."

(Matthew 11:12) "From the days of John the Baptist until now the kingdom of heaven has suffered violence, and men of violence take it by force."

wicked. But thou, my soul, hast followed the second of these, not the first, and hast sinned against God.

Have mercy on me, O God, have mercy on me.

339. The Law is powerless, the gospel of no effect, and the whole of Scripture is ignored by thee; the prophets and all the words of the righteous are useless. Thy wounds, my soul, have been multiplied, and there is no physician to heal thee.

Have mercy on me, O God, have mercy on me.

340. I bring thee, O my soul, examples from the New Testament, to lead thee to compunction. Follow the example of the righteous, turn away from the sinful; and through prayers and fasting, through chastity and reverence, win back Christ's mercy.

Have mercy on me, O God, have mercy on me.

341. Christ became a child and shared in my flesh; and willingly He performed all that belongs to my nature, only without sin. He set before thee, my soul, an example and image of His condescension.

Have mercy on me, O God, have mercy on me.

342. Christ became man, calling to repentance thieves and harlots. Repent, my soul: the door of the kingdom is already open, and Pharisees and publicans and adulterers pass through it before thee, changing their lives.

Have mercy on me, O God, have mercy on me.

343. **"Saved the wise men."** (Matthew 2:12) The wise men were warned in a dream not to return to Herod.

"Called the shepherds." (Luke 2:8–18) Angels appeared to shepherds in the field and told them of the birth of Jesus.

"Revealed as martyrs a multitude of young children." (Matthew 2:16) Herod, attempting to kill the newborn Jesus, "in a furious rage . . . sent and killed all the male children in Bethlehem and in all that region who were two years old or under."

"Glorified the elder and the aged widow." (Luke 2:25–38) When Mary and Joseph came to the temple to make the appointed offering for a newborn son, they were met by the aged Simeon, who prophesied over the child. A widow, Anna, a prophetess who "did not depart from the temple, worshiping with fasting and prayer night and day," came up at the same time and also proclaimed the news of Christ's birth.

344. **"He was hungry."** (Matthew 4:1-2) "Jesus was led up by the Spirit into the wilderness to be tempted by the devil. And he fasted forty days and forty nights, and afterward he was hungry." His hunger shows that He was human like we are, and susceptible to the same bodily needs.

"Through prayer and fasting drive him away." (Matthew 17:21) "But this kind [of demon] never comes out except by prayer and fasting."

345. **"The devil tempted Him."** (Matthew 4:3–11) In the wilderness the devil tempts Christ to satisfy His hunger by turning stones to bread, and offers to give Him all the kingdoms of the world in return for worship.

CONSIDER

Verse 341 gives us encouragement. When Christ took on human nature, He took on everything that belongs to us, even our vulnerability to temptation. This comforting thought became obscured in Western Christian theology due to the teaching that He, and His mother the Theotokos, were born "without stain of original sin." This concept of inherited guilt was developed by Augustine of Hippo (354–430 AD), and although it was powerfully influential in Western Europe, it was never accepted in the Christian East. (Nor had it been part of the Jewish understanding of their own Scriptures; the idea did not appear before Augustine.)

343. Christ saved the wise men and called the shepherds; He revealed as martyrs a multitude of young children; He glorified the elder and the aged widow. But thou, my soul, hast not followed their lives and actions. Woe to thee when thou art judged!

Have mercy on me, O God, have mercy on me.

344. The Lord fasted forty days in the wilderness, and at the end of them He was hungry, thus showing that He is man. Do not be dismayed, my soul: if the enemy attacks thee, through prayer and fasting drive him away.

Have mercy on me, O God, have mercy on me.

345. Christ was being tempted; the devil tempted Him, showing Him the stones that they might be made bread. He led Him up into a mountain, to see in an instant all the kingdoms of the world. O my soul, look with fear on what happened; watch and pray every hour to God.

Have mercy on me, O God, have mercy on me.

Of course, every human is damaged by the sin of Adam and Eve, and is born with, so to speak, a spiritual "broken gene." We have a hereditary instability that makes us powerfully drawn to sin. The reassuring message of Hebrews 4:15 is that Christ was born with the exact same nature we are. He didn't have a secret advantage of being born without "original sin" (nor did His Mother). He had to struggle along with the same moral equipment we have, submitting His human will to the will of the Father, out of love and obedience. Not only does this example give us hope, but it reminds us that He knows what we're going through. He can sympathize with us. (Hebrews 4:16) "Let us then with confidence draw near to the throne of grace, that we may receive mercy and find grace to help in time of need."

COMMENTARY

CHAPTER 38

EXPLORE

346. **"The dove who loved the wilderness.":** St. John the Forerunner. (Psalm 55:6-7) "And I say, 'O that I had wings like a dove! I would fly away and be at rest; yea, I would wander afar, I would lodge in the wilderness.'"

"The lamp of Christ." (John 5:35) Jesus says of John, "He was a burning and shining lamp, and you were willing to rejoice for a while in his light."

"The voice of one crying aloud." (Isaiah 40:3) "A voice cries: 'In the wilderness prepare the way of the LORD, make straight in the desert a highway for our God.'"

"Heard preaching repentance." (Matthew 3:2) John came preaching, "Repent, for the kingdom of heaven is at hand."

"But Herod sinned with Herodias," despite hearing St. John's call to repentance. Herod formed an adulterous union with his niece Herodias, who had been married to his brother Philip. St. John the Forerunner preached publicly against this, prompting Herod to imprison him. However, in prison Herod began to visit St. John and listen to him. "When he heard him, he was much perplexed; and yet he heard him gladly" (Mark 6:20b). Herod reluctantly had St. John beheaded, after being caught in a promise he was embarrassed to break.

CHAPTER 38

346. The dove who loved the wilderness, the lamp of Christ, the voice of one crying aloud, was heard preaching repentance; but Herod sinned with Herodias. O my soul, see that thou art not trapped in the snares of the transgressors, but embrace repentance.

Have mercy on me, O God, have mercy on me.

"Not trapped in the snares." (Psalm 124:7) "We have escaped as a bird from the snare of the fowlers; the snare is broken, and we have escaped!"

347. **"Judaea and all Samaria ran to hear him."** (Matthew 3:5-6) "Then went out to him Jerusalem and all Judea and all the region about the Jordan, and they were baptized by him in the river Jordan, confessing their sins."

348. **"Marriage is honorable."** (Hebrews 13:4) "Let marriage be held in honor among all, and let the marriage bed be undefiled." **"At the wedding in Cana."** (John 2:1–11). Christ's first miracle was at a wedding in the village of Cana. They ran out of wine at the feast, so Christ had the servants fill six stone jars with water, then told the steward of the feast to draw some out and taste it. It had become excellent wine—superior to that which had been previously served. Each of the jars held twenty or thirty gallons, so it was an immense quantity of wine.

349. **"Strength to the paralyzed man."** (Matthew 9:2–7) Christ heals a paralytic after his friends lower him through the roof.

"Raised from the dead the young man" (Luke 7:11–15) Christ stops a funeral procession and raises the young man from the dead. A widow who lost her only son would have no means of support.

"And the centurion's servant." (Matthew 8:5–13) The centurion was a Roman military officer, and thus not an Israelite. But he had confidence that Christ could heal his paralyzed servant with a word, without even coming to his house. Christ said, "Not even in Israel have I found such faith."

"Worship in spirit." (John 4:24) Christ told the Samaritan woman He met at the well, "God is spirit, and those who worship him must worship in spirit and truth."

350. **"Touch of the hem."** (Mark 5:25–34) A woman is healed by coming up in a crowd and touching Christ's garment.

"Cleansed lepers." (Matthew 11:4-5) Christ sends word to St. John that He is doing these works: "[T]he blind receive their sight and the lame walk, lepers are cleansed and the deaf hear, and the dead are raised up, and the poor have good news preached to them."

347. The forerunner of grace went to dwell in the wilderness, and Judea and all Samaria ran to hear him; they confessed their sins and were baptized eagerly. But thou, my soul, hast not imitated them.

Have mercy on me, O God, have mercy on me.

348. Marriage is honorable, and the marriage bed undefiled. For on both Christ has given His blessing, eating in the flesh at the wedding in Cana, turning water into wine and revealing His first miracle, to bring thee, my soul, to a change of life.

Have mercy on me, O God, have mercy on me.

349. Christ gave strength to the paralyzed man, and he took up his bed; He raised from the dead the young man, the son of the widow, and the centurion's servant; He appeared to the woman of Samaria, and spoke to thee, my soul, of worship in spirit.

Have mercy on me, O God, have mercy on me.

350. By the touch of the hem of His garment, the Lord healed the woman with an issue of blood; He cleansed lepers and gave sight to the blind and made the lame walk upright; He cured by His word the deaf and the dumb and the woman bowed to the ground, to bring thee, wretched soul, to salvation.

Have mercy on me, O God, have mercy on me.

"**Woman bowed to the ground.**" (Luke 13:11–13) A woman had been bowed down for eighteen years. Christ "laid his hands upon her, and immediately she was made straight, and she praised God."

351. "**Preached the good tidings.**" (Luke 4:17–19) In the synagogue at Nazareth, Christ reads Isaiah 61:1, "The Spirit of the Lord is upon me, because he has anointed me to preach good news to the poor."

"**Ate with publicans.**" (Luke 5:27–29) When Christ saw Levi the tax-collector, He said, "Follow me." Levi (later named Matthew) made a great feast for Christ.

"**Brought back the departed soul of Jairus's daughter.**" (Mark 5:22–43) This twelve-year-old girl was lying dead on her bed when Christ took her hand and said, "Little girl, arise."

352. "**Publican was saved.**" (Luke 18:14a) The tax-collector humbly begged God for mercy. "I tell you, this man went down to his house justified."

"**Harlot turned to chastity.**" (Luke 7:48, 50) The woman washed Christ's feet with her tears. "[H]e said to her, 'Your sins are forgiven . . . Your faith has saved you; go in peace.'"

"**The third said, boasting.**" (Luke 18:11) The Pharisee, seeing the tax-collector in the temple, mentally compared himself with the wealthy lackey of Rome. He thanked God that he was sexually pure, fasted strenuously, and gave ten percent of all his income to charity. For this boasting he was condemned.

CONSIDER

St. Andrew repeatedly emphasizes that these events and passages in Scripture are written to him personally. Christ's words to the woman of Samaria about worship in spirit are, St. Andrew feels, spoken directly to him. Christ's first miracle, when water was changed into wine, was done "**to bring thee, my soul, to a changed life.**" In every passage of Scripture, God is reaching out to him personally.

We can fall into the habit of picturing the Scriptures as a big important book that is floating majestically in space, saying important things to nobody in particular. But the Scriptures mean nothing until they connect with an individual person's receptive mind and heart. Then a spark of energy flies out, as when an electric circuit is completed. Each story and teaching of Scripture

351. Healing sickness, Christ the Word preached the good tidings to the poor. He cured the crippled, ate with publicans, and conversed with sinners. With the touch of His hand, He brought back the departed soul of Jairus's daughter.

Have mercy on me, O God, have mercy on me.

352. The publican was saved and the harlot turned to chastity, but the Pharisee with his boasting was condemned. For the first cried, "Be merciful," and the second, "Have mercy on me"; but the third said, boasting, "I thank Thee, O God," and the other words of madness.

Have mercy on me, O God, have mercy on me.

is something God is whispering in your ear—to you, personally—
and until you respond it might as well not exist. Are there
Scriptures that "speak" to you with particular strength? Are
there Scriptures that confuse or frustrate you? Be alert to those
Scriptures that offend you, for that is often a sign of a place to
grow. Which of the incidents from Christ's life that St. Andrew
mentions in this section are calling to you most strongly today?

COMMENTARY
CHAPTER 39

EXPLORE

353. **"Zacchaeus was a publican, yet he was saved."** (Luke 19:2–10)
Zacchaeus was a chief tax-collector in Jericho. He was short of
stature, and, as Jesus passed by, could not see Him because of
the crowds. He climbed up into a sycamore tree—a ridiculous
position for an unpopular businessman. But as Jesus passed
beneath it He stopped, looked up, and said to Zacchaeus:
"[C]ome down, I must stay at your house today." Zacchaeus
joyfully made a feast for Jesus, and told Him that he would
restore everything he had extorted four times over, and would
give half of his goods to the poor. Jesus told him, "Today salvation
has come to this house" (Luke 19:9).

  "Simon the Pharisee went astray." (Luke 7:36–50) While Jesus
was at dinner at Simon's house the harlot came in to weep at his
feet. Jesus pointed out to Simon that, though the sinful woman
had given extravagantly, he as host had not offered even the
customary hospitality. Simon did not feel himself in need of
God's mercy, and as a result did not feel grateful love.

354. **"The harlot."** The figure in the above story (Luke 7:36–50).

  "Tore in pieces the record of her sins." (Colossians 2:14) God
"canceled the bond which stood against us with its legal
demands; this He set aside, nailing it to the cross."

355. **"The cities were cursed."** (Matthew 11:23-24) Christ said that
cities where He preached which did not respond to Him would
suffer. "And you, Capernaum, will you be exalted to heaven? You
shall be brought down to Hades. For if the mighty works done in
you had been done in Sodom, it would have remained until this
day. But I tell you that it shall be more tolerable on the day of
judgment for the land of Sodom than for you."

CHAPTER 39

353. Zacchaeus was a publican, yet he was saved; but Simon the Pharisee went astray, while the harlot received remission and release from Him who has the power to forgive sins. O my soul, gain His mercy.

Have mercy on me, O God, have mercy on me.

354. O wretched soul, thou hast not acted like the harlot, who took the alabaster box of precious ointment, and anointed with tears and wiped with her hair the feet of the Lord. And He tore in pieces the record of her previous sins.

Have mercy on me, O God, have mercy on me.

355. Thou knowest, O my soul, how the cities were cursed to which Christ preached the gospel. Fear their example, lest thou suffer the same punishment. For the Master likened them to Sodom and condemned them to hell.

Have mercy on me, O God, have mercy on me.

356. **"Faith of the woman of Canaan."** (Matthew 15:22–28) As Christ passed through the region of Tyre, a Canaanite woman begged him to heal her demon-possessed daughter. Although she was not an Israelite, He did so because of the strength of her faith.

357. **"Thou hast healed the possessed."** A high proportion of Christ's healings were of people possessed by demons. St. Andrew asks to be delivered from the evil one who takes us captive by our sins.

"Let me hear Thy compassionate voice." (Luke 23:42-43) The good thief said, "'Jesus, remember me when you come into your kingdom.' And he said to him, 'Truly, I say to you, today you will be with me in Paradise.'"

358. **"A thief accused Thee."** (Luke 23:39) The other thief crucified with Jesus screamed at Him to use His supposed superpowers to rescue them all. "One of the criminals who were hanged railed at him, saying, 'Are you not the Christ? Save yourself and us!'"

359. **"The creation was in anguish."** (Matthew 27:51-52) "[T]he curtain of the temple was torn in two, from top to bottom; and the earth shook, and the rocks were split; the tombs also were opened, and many bodies of the saints who had fallen asleep were raised."

(Luke 23:44-45a) "[T]here was darkness over the whole land until the ninth hour, while the sun's light failed."

CONSIDER

In Romans 8:19–23, St. Paul speaks about the anguish of the created world. It is "in bondage to decay" and "subjected to futility." The world was created beautiful and good, and Adam and Eve were placed over it as leaders. But when they fell into sin, creation was left leaderless and crumpled as well, experiencing violence, meaninglessness, and death. "[T]he whole creation has been groaning in travail until now."

Yet there is hope. "The creation waits for eager longing for the revealing of the sons of God." When the sons and daughters of Adam and Eve are restored to communion with God as His children, creation will be restored as well. The end point is the resurrection of all humankind at the end of history, when the dead are raised and these mortal bodies are transformed to be like Christ's resurrection body. (Romans 8:23) "[N]ot only the creation, but we ourselves, who have the first fruits of the Spirit, groan inwardly as we wait for adoption as sons, the redemption of our bodies."

356. Be not overcome by despair, O my soul; for thou hast heard of the faith of the woman of Canaan, and how through it her daughter was healed by the word of God. Cry out from the depth of thy heart, "Save me also, Son of David," as she once cried to Christ.

Have mercy on me, O God, have mercy on me.

357. O Son of David, with Thy word Thou hast healed the possessed: Take pity on me, save me and have mercy. Let me hear Thy compassionate voice speak to me as to the thief: "Verily, I say unto thee, thou shalt be with Me in paradise, when I come in My glory."

Have mercy on me, O God, have mercy on me.

358. A thief accused Thee, a thief confessed Thy Godhead: for both were hanging with Thee on the cross. Open to me also, O Lord of many mercies, the door of Thy glorious kingdom, as once it was opened to the thief who acknowledged Thee with faith as God.

Have mercy on me, O God, have mercy on me.

359. The creation was in anguish, seeing Thee crucified. Mountains and rocks were split from fear, the earth quaked, and hell was despoiled; the light grew dark in daytime, beholding Thee, O Jesus, nailed in the flesh.

Have mercy on me, O God, have mercy on me.

We're inclined to forget about our bodies; we think that faith has to do with "spiritual" things. But the early Christians understood that the human person is a unity composed of physical, mental, emotional, and spiritual elements, and the separation of the body from the rest is both unnatural and temporary. One day, the very body you have right now, including the bones in your fingers holding this book, will be raised from the dead and revealed in its final form. "Beloved, we are God's children now; it does not yet appear what we shall be, but we know that when he appears we shall be like him, for we shall see him as he is" (1 John 3:2). There is no part of you that does not belong to God, and that will not be transformed to "be like Him." As you pray today, offer your whole body as a temple of the Holy Spirit (1 Corinthians 6:19).

COMMENTARY
CHAPTER 40

EXPLORE

360. **"Worthy fruits of repentance."** (Matthew 3:8) St. John the Forerunner said, "Bear fruit that befits repentance."

"Ever-contrite heart." (Psalm 51:17) "The sacrifice acceptable to God is a broken spirit; a broken and contrite heart, O God, thou wilt not despise."

"Poverty of spirit." (Matthew 5:3) "Blessed are the poor in spirit, for theirs is the kingdom of heaven."

361. **"When Thou comest again with the angels."** (Matthew 25:31) "When the Son of man comes in his glory, and all the angels with him, then he will sit on his glorious throne."

362. **"Thou hast surpassed nature."** A person wholly filled with the presence of Christ will be able to do the works He did, such as walk on water (Matthew 14:25). "Truly, truly, I say to you, he who believes in me will also do the works that I do; and greater works than these will he do, because I go to the Father" (John 14:12).

363. **"Sufferings and afflictions that assail us . . . delivered from temptations."** Suffering and affliction can weaken our resistance to temptation. St. Mary of Egypt's prayers are powerful: "[P]ray for one another, that you may be healed. The prayer of a righteous man has great power in its effects" (James 5:16).

CHAPTER 40

360. Do not demand from me worthy fruits of repentance, for my strength has failed within me. Give me an ever-contrite heart and poverty of spirit, that I may offer these to Thee as an acceptable sacrifice, O only Savior.

Have mercy on me, O God, have mercy on me.

361. O my Judge who dost know me, when Thou comest again with the angels to judge the whole world, look upon me then with Thine eye of mercy, and spare me; take pity on me, Jesus, for I have sinned more than any other man.

Holy Mother Mary, pray to God for us.

362. By thy strange way of life thou hast struck all with wonder, both the hosts of angels and the gatherings of mortal men; for thou hast surpassed nature and lived as though no longer in the body. Like a bodiless angel thou hast walked upon the Jordan with thy feet, O Mary, and crossed over it.

Holy Mother Mary, pray to God for us.

363. O holy Mother, call down the gracious mercy of the Creator upon us who sing thy praises, that we may be set free from the sufferings and afflictions that assail us; so without ceasing, delivered from temptations, we shall magnify the Lord who has glorified thee.

364. St. Andrew's prayers, likewise, deliver us not only from **"danger and distress,"** but also assist in helping us escape **"innumerable sins."**

366. **"Putting to flight every temptation, despoiling the enemy."** And lastly we call on the prayers of the Virgin Mary, which are powerful to deliver us from the evil one and his assaults.

CONSIDER

As the Great Canon comes to a conclusion, we find ourselves surrounded by a powerful array of angels and saints, new friends who intercede for us and protect us by their prayers. If we have been praying through this great hymn attentively, we arrive at the end less sure of ourselves, less confident, and more sensitive to our weakness in resisting the things that drag us away from God. And yet we can be more confident in God's mercy; we have less to worry about, in terms of "keeping up a good front" of holiness, and more tranquility in the assurance of God's complete knowledge of us, inside and out, and His unceasing will to rescue and save us.

This is a path that goes on forever. If the prayer of St. Andrew has taken root in you, and you are beginning to "catch" the way life in Christ was envisioned by the early church, you can progress every day a little farther: every day seeing more of your own sins, every day losing more confidence in your homemade excellence, every day drinking deeper of the cup of humility. And as humility increases, so does joy, because you can let go of false fronts, and know yourself loved exactly the way you are. God will not leave you the way you are; His will is to make you like He is. "You, therefore, must be perfect, as your heavenly Father is perfect" (Matthew 5:48). This is a lifelong journey, but not one you have to make alone. The friends you have met as you have prayed through this hymn will be with you all your life—and beyond.

Holy Father Andrew, pray to God for us.

364. Venerable Andrew, father thrice-blessed, shepherd of Crete, cease not to offer prayer for us who sing thy praises; that we may be delivered from all danger and distress, from corruption and innumerable sins, who honor thy memory with faith.

Glory to the Father, and to the Son, and to the Holy Spirit.

365. Trinity, one in Essence, Unity in three Persons, we sing Thy praises: We glorify the Father, we magnify the Son, we worship the Spirit, truly one God by nature, Life and Lives, kingdom without end.

Both now and ever and unto ages of ages. Amen.

366. Watch over thy city, all-pure Mother of God. For by thee she reigns in faith, by thee she is made strong; by thee she is victorious, putting to flight every temptation, despoiling the enemy and ruling her subjects.

367. Conception without seed; nativity past understanding, from a Mother who never knew a man; childbearing undefiled. For the birth of God makes both natures new. Therefore, as Bride and Mother of God, with true worship all generations magnify thee.

Appendix

The Life of St. Mary of Egypt

St. Mary of Egypt lived approximately two hundred years before St. Andrew wrote his Canon, and in that time her story had become well-loved. Many verses in the Canon ask for her prayers. At the Lenten service in which the Canon is chanted in its fullness, the first half of her life story is read before beginning the Canon, and the second at the end of the Third Canticle.

The life of St. Mary of Egypt was written down by St. Sophronius of Jerusalem in the seventh century. I have shortened and paraphrased his work, while attempting not to alter or add anything. The full version is readily available on the Internet.

First Reading

It is necessary to proclaim the great deeds of God, and not be like the servant who hid the talent in the ground. With that in mind this story is here presented, and the elements of it can be considered reliable, because the informant was "a pious man who, from childhood, has instructed himself in divine words and acts." Some may find these miraculous events hard to believe, assuming that "it is impossible in our generation to work such wonders." But "the grace of the Father, flowing from generation to generation," does not end.

The story begins with a monk named Zosimas, who had pursued growth in Christ from his infancy. He excelled in the ascetic struggle, followed all the instructions given by

181

his spiritual fathers, and "had thought out much on his own, laboring to submit the flesh to the spirit. . . . And he did not miss his goal." His chief love was reading the Scriptures, which he found ways to do even while "resting, standing, working, or eating food (if the scraps he nibbled could be called food)." He had advanced so far that he was becoming well-known, and monks from monasteries "both near and far" came to hear his teaching.

But when Zosimas was fifty-three years old, "thoughts began to torment him." He began to think that he was the most advanced monk alive, and that there was no one left who could teach him anything. An angel appeared to him and told him that, though he had done admirably, "before you lie unknown struggles greater than those you have accomplished." The angel told Zosimas to leave his present monastery and move to a different one, near the Jordan River.

This Zosimas did, and on the banks of the Jordan he found a community of monks who had advanced far in the angelic life. There Zosimas "was wholly edified, and ran forward all the faster, for he had found himself fellow workers who renewed with art the garden of God."

Many days later the time of Lent drew near. There was a custom in this monastery that was the reason God brought Zosimas there. On the first day of Lent, a Sunday, there was as usual a morning Eucharist, and then the monks would have a small Lenten meal. After this they gathered again in the church and, one by one, embraced and kissed each other, bowing to the ground and asking each other's forgiveness for any offenses. (This Rite of Forgiveness is still observed in Orthodox congregations at vespers the first day of Lent.) The monks asked each other to be, during this time of heightened ascetic struggle, a "fellow fighter and fellow worker during the battle at hand."

Then the monks set out into the desert. "The gates of the monastery were thrown open, and singing 'The Lord is my light and my Savior; whom shall I fear?'" they left the enclosure behind and, crossing the Jordan, "scattered far and wide in different directions." For the next six weeks they would avoid any contact with each other, so that their discipline of prayer and fasting would be unobserved, free from any motivation by pride. On Palm Sunday "each one returned, having his own conscience as the witness of his labor, and no one asked another how he had spent his time in the desert."

Zosimas eagerly took up this discipline, and as he walked along an idea "fell into his soul" suggesting that he might meet some spiritual giant in the wilderness. This idea began "pushing him to go deeper and deeper into the desert," and he began to hurry, as if seeking to arrive at some inn he knew. He had been traveling in this way for twenty days, going ever deeper into the wilderness, when he stopped one day for the customary prayers. Turning toward the east, Zosimas dropped to his knees and began singing the noon-time psalms.

But then he glimpsed something like a shadow on a hillock to his right. As his prayers ended, he turned and saw the figure of a human being, walking away to the south. "This being was naked, its body blackened, burnt by the heat of the sun; the hair on its head was white as fleece and not long, descending no lower than the neck."

Zosimas was overjoyed; in all these days he had not seen another human, or even a bird or beast. He "hoped that some mighty mysteries" would now be revealed to him. He began to run toward the figure but, no doubt to his surprise, it ran swiftly away—so swiftly that Zosimas could hardly keep up. He begged it with tears, "Wait for me, true servant of God, whoever you may be, I beseech you in the name of God, for whose sake you live in this desert."

They came to a stop in a place the looked like a dried-up riverbed. The figure then called out, "Abba Zosimas, forgive me, I cannot turn around. I am a woman, and my body in uncovered shame is naked." Zosimas was frightened; how could she know his name? She must have a divine gift of knowledge. She then asked Zosimas to throw her his cloak, and when he did so, she covered herself and came back to him.

"Why, Father Zosimas, have you desired to see a sinful woman?" she asked him. "What do you wish to know, that you would take on yourself such hard labor?"

At this Zosimas fell to his knees and asked her to bless him, but the aged desert-dweller immediately did the same. She reminded him, "It is fit for you to bless, Abba Zosimas. You have the rank of priest and for many years have stood before the altar of God." Zosimas was yet more terrified that she would know he was a priest, since not all monks are ordained.

"Finally, getting back his breath with difficulty," Zosimas insisted on her blessing, which she gave. When they stood, she asked him how things were going in the world, and he replied, "By your prayers, Mother, Christ has given peace to all." He then asked her to pray "for the whole world and for me, a sinner." Again she reminded Zosimas that it was his place, as a priest, to pray. Yet at his request she turned to the east, and lifting her eyes and her hands to heaven, began to pray.

She spoke very softly, in a whisper. Zosimas could not understand the words. He stood trembling and looking at the ground. But "when at length he thought that her prayer was very long," he glanced over at her. When he recounted this story to his fellow monks later on, he insisted, "calling God to witness," that she was raised about an arm's length from the earth and stood praying in the air. "He fell on the ground in a sweat and terrified, simply repeating over and over, 'Lord, have mercy.'"

While he was cowering there, another thought crept into his mind. Might she be an evil spirit? Might the unheard prayer be fraudulent? Immediately the woman turned around and pulled him to his feet. "Why do thoughts confuse you, Abba, and tempt you about me, as if I were a spirit and liar in prayer?" she asked. "Know that I am a sinful woman, not a spirit but earth and ashes." She made the sign of the cross on her forehead, eyes, mouth, and breast. "May God deliver us from the evil one and from his snares," she said.

Zosimas could take no more. He fell to the ground again, and laying hold of her feet, begged her with tears to tell him who she was. "I believe that God, for whom you live and whom you serve," he said, "brought me to this desert in order to make plain the ways of the Lord concerning you." If God had not wanted Zosimas to meet her and learn her story, "He would not have let me see anybody, and He would not have given me strength to take such a journey."

Once again the woman lifted him to his feet. "I am ashamed, my Abba, to tell you of my deeds," she said. "It is not from vainglory," as one might boast of ascetic exploits; "about what should I be vainglorious, having

185

been the chosen vessel of the devil? I know that when I shall begin my story, you will flee from me, and your ears will be unable to hear the foulness of my deeds. But I shall declare them, beseeching you to pray without ceasing for me."

Zosimas by now was weeping uncontrollably. The woman began her story.

SECOND READING

"My native land was Egypt," she said. "While my parents were still alive, when I was only twelve years old, I rejected their love and went to Alexandria. When I remember how I lost my virginity there at the beginning, how I unrestrainedly and insatiably gave myself up to lust, it makes me ashamed." Insatiability seems to have been the keynote of this young woman's passion. She told Zosimas that, for seventeen years, she lived in Alexandria, seeking every possible kind of sexual experience. She was not a prostitute: "Often, when people wanted to give me money, I refused. I lived off charity, and weaving flax." Her goal was to provoke "as many people as possible" to desire her, "doing for nothing what gave me pleasure." She found various perversions particularly delightful. "I had an unrestrainable passion to wallow in the mud. This was life for me. I held in honor every outrage to nature."

One summer day she saw a crowd of people heading toward the docks. When she asked, she was told that they were boarding a ship for Jerusalem, to attend the feast of the Exaltation of the Cross; every year, on September 13, the cross that had been uncovered by St. Helena in her fourth-century excavation was held up for all to venerate.

The woman decided to go along with them, offering her body as payment: "Forgive me, Abba, so as to have as many lovers as possible."

She ran toward the sea, "throwing away the spindle I carried with me in those days. Seeing some young men, about ten or more, standing on the beach full of strength and supple of movement, I found them suitable for my purposes. 'Take me with you on your journey,' I said, 'and I will not be a burden to you.'" She added a bit more, making her meaning explicit, and they gladly took her on board.

"How shall I tell you, man of God, what happened next?" The woman taught the young men every "mentionable or unmentionable depravity," and "frequently forced those miserable youths, even against their own will." She wonders why the sea did not simply swallow them up. "But I think that God sought my repentance. For He does not want the death of a sinner, but waits, great-heartedly, for him to return."

The ship docked and the passengers made their way to Jerusalem, where the woman continued her exploits. When the day of the feast arrived "I was still flying about, hunting for youths" among both citizens of the town and strangers.

At dawn on the feast she saw people heading toward the Church of the Holy Sepulchre and joined them. It was very crowded, and once she had entered the building she had difficulty working her way through the foyer to the door that led into the church. She was about to step in, "but when I trod on the doorstep which everyone passed, I was stopped by some force which prevented me entering." Others pushed past her, and she found herself once again shoved back into the narthex. "Thinking that this had happened to me because of my womanly weakness, I began to edge my way along with my elbows." But once again she stood still at the doorway of the church. "It was as if a detachment of soldiers were standing there to oppose my entrance." She tried three or four times to enter the church, until she was exhausted and "had no more strength to push or be pushed."

She went off and stood in a corner. "And little by little I began to understand the reason why I was being prevented from looking on the life-bearing cross of the Lord. The word of salvation gently touched my heart, and revealed to me that it was my unclean life which barred the entrance to me."

Tears sprang into her eyes, and began to wash away long years of degradation and misery. She saw in the corner an icon of the Virgin Mary. She prayed, "Virgin Lady, I know, O how well I know, that it is no honor to thee when one so depraved as I look up to thy icon. But I have heard that God who was born of thee became man on purpose to call sinners to repentance. Then help me, for I have no other help." She asked to be allowed to enter the church and look on the cross, and promised that afterward "I will renounce the world and its temptations, and go wherever thou wilt lead me."

This time when she approached the door of the church she was able to step in. "I was possessed with trembling, almost in delirium." She continued to the holy place "and so it was that I saw the life-giving cross. I saw the mysteries of God, and how the Lord accepts repentance." Returning to the icon of the Virgin, she knelt and asked to be led forward. She heard a voice saying, "If you cross the Jordan, you will find glorious rest."

As she set out from the church someone stopped her and, saying "Take these, little mother," gave her three silver coins. She bought three loaves of bread, and asking directions along the way, finally came to the Jordan River about sunset. At the nearby Church of St. John the Forerunner she received Communion, then spent the night on the ground. The next day she crossed the river, and began her sojourn in the wilderness.

"How many years have passed that you lived in the desert?" Zosimas asked.

"It seems to me that it is forty-seven years since I went out of the Holy City," she replied.

Zosimas next asked her what she had eaten all this time, and she replied, "I had two and a half loaves when I crossed the Jordan, which soon became dried up like stones. Eating them little by little I finished them after a few years."

Zosimas asked in astonishment, "Is it possible that you lived in the desert for so many years, without suffering from such a complete change of life?"

The woman told Zosimas that she was afraid to talk about this, for fear that "all the violent thoughts which confused me will again take possession of me." Zosimas begged her to hold nothing back.

"Believe me, Abba, seventeen years I spent in this desert fighting 'wild beasts'—my mad desires and passions." Whenever she felt hungry, she would long for the meat and fish of Egypt. "I regretted also not having wine, which I loved so much. For I drank a lot of wine when I lived in the world, and here I had not even water." Tormented by hunger and thirst, she would also remember the songs that used to accompany her carousing, and feel a strong desire to burst out in song. She would weep loudly and cry for help to the Virgin Theotokos, and recall her appearance in the icon. "I implored her to chase away the thoughts that overwhelmed my miserable soul. And when I had wept enough, I used to see a light that illumined me on all sides. And finally, after the clamor, fell a long period of quiet."

She likewise was tormented by sexual cravings. "Fire burned in my unhappy heart and it consumed me entirely." She learned to throw herself to the ground immediately, weeping and "seeing before me the Virgin who had gone security for me," who now seemed to be chastising her. She would continue in prayer until "that sweet light that had enlightened me had chased away the thoughts that raged in me." She continually begged the Virgin for help "as I sank in the waves of the desert." After seventeen years these struggles abated. From that time the Virgin had always been near her as a defender, and "leads me by the hand."

Zosimas asked, "Have you really not wanted for food and clothing?" She replied that, during those initial seventeen years, she consumed the loaves bit by bit, and also fed on whatever desert plants she came across. Her clothes gradually wore out, and then her naked body, which had once been her joy, was burned by the sun and frozen by the desert night. At times she "lay on the ground without breath or movement," seeming to hover between life and death. But she learned to be fed by "the hope of salvation" and "clothed by the word of God, for man does not live by bread alone."

When Zosimas heard her quote from Scripture he asked her whether she had read the Bible. She smiled as she replied, "Believe me, I have not see a human face since I crossed the

Jordan, until yours today. I have not seen a beast or a living thing. I never learned from books. But the Word of God Himself, alive and active, teaches a person knowledge."

She then asked Zosimas again to pray for her, and bowed before him. He exclaimed, "Blessed is God, who has done great and wondrous things, glorious and marvelous, that cannot be numbered! Blessed is God, Who hath shown me how He rewards those who fear Him! Truly, O Lord, Thou dost not forsake those who seek Thee!"

He moved to bow before her, but she stopped him. "I beg you, father, to tell no one what you have heard, until God delivers me from this earth. And now depart in peace, and next year you will see me again. But when Lent begins, do not cross the Jordan, as is the custom in the monastery." Zosimas again was struck with wonder, that she knew the rule of his monastery. She went on, "Remain in the monastery. Even if you wish to depart, you will not be able to do so. But at sunset on the holy day of the Last Supper"—the Thursday before Easter—"put some of the life-giving Body and Blood of Christ into a worthy vessel and bring it, and wait for me on the banks of the Jordan." She told Zosimas that she had not received the Eucharistic Gifts since the day she set out for the wilderness, and she thirsted for it with insatiable longing.

She went on, "Tell John, the abbot of your monastery, 'Look to your flock; something is happening in your monastery that needs amendment.' Don't say this to him now, but at the time that the Lord will show you." And with a final, "Pray for me," she vanished into the desert. Zosimas knelt at the spot where her feet had stood and prayed, then began the long journey back to his monastery.

The following year was a struggle for Zosimas. He didn't dare tell anyone what he had seen, and he longed to see the old woman's face again. "He tormented himself and worried himself to pieces, thinking about how long a year is, and wishing that the year be shortened into a single day." At last the first Sunday of the Holy Fast came again, but when all the monks went out singing psalms, Zosimas was sick in bed with a fever and could not go with them, just as she had said. Slowly the weeks passed, and the monks returned in time for Palm Sunday and Holy Week.

When Holy Thursday came, Zosimas did as the woman had asked; he took a portion of the Holy Gifts and put them in a basket with some figs and dates, and a small quantity of lentils. Late that night he set out for the Jordan. When he reached the river he could not find her anywhere, and sat down to wait on the riverbank, feeling worried. It was a clear, moonlit night. Zosimas thought, "Either my unworthiness prevented her coming, or she came and, not finding me, went back again." He started weeping and cried out to God, "O Master, let me again behold the sight Thou hast allowed me to behold once."

Then fresh doubts assailed him. "And what if she does come? There is no boat; how will she cross the Jordan?"

While he was thinking this she appeared on the far side of the river. She made the sign of the cross upon the water, then stepped onto it and began walking toward him on the waves. Zosimas began to make a prostration before her, but she stood still on the water and scolded him. "What are you doing, Abba? You are a priest, and you are carrying the Divine Gifts!"

As she stepped onto the bank Zosimas exclaimed, "Truly God is no liar, when He promised that those who purify themselves shall be like Him. Glory to Thee, O Christ our God, who hast shown me through Thy servant how far I am from perfection."

She asked Zosimas to pray the Nicene Creed and the Our Father, and when he began, she joined him. She then gave him the kiss of peace and received the Holy Mysteries. She raised her arms to heaven and sighed with tears, praying, "Lord, now lettest Thou Thy servant depart in peace, according to Thy word, for mine eyes have seen Thy salvation."

She then said to Zosimas, "Forgive me, Abba, for asking you, but please fulfill another wish of mine. Return now to the monastery, and come again next year to the riverbed where I first met you. You will see me again, for such is the will of God."

Zosimas burst out, "I would like to follow you every day and always see your holy face." He offered her the basket of food, but she only touched the lentils with her fingertips and raised three grains to her mouth, saying "the Holy Spirit is sufficient to keep the nature of the soul undefiled." She told Zosimas, "Pray, for God's sake, pray for me, and remember me, a miserable wretch."

Seeing that he could not persuade her to allow him to follow her, Zosimas let her go, having made many requests for her prayers. He saw that "he had no hope of overcoming the unconquerable." She made the sign of the cross on the waters and stepped onto them, crossing once again to the desert. Zosimas returned to the monastery full of joy and awe, and reproached himself that he had forgotten to ask her name.

A year passed, and this time Zosimas eagerly went into the desert and sought the dried riverbed where he had first met the aged woman. He could not see her anywhere, and prayed, "Show me, O Master, Thy pure treasure, the angel in the flesh, of whom the world is not worthy."

Then he saw her body lying dead. "Her hands were crossed according to custom and her face was turned toward the east."

Zosimas ran to her and wept over her, and recited the appointed psalms. Then he noticed some words written into the ground near her head: "O Abba Zosimas, bury on this spot the body of humble Mary. Return dust to dust, and pray to the Lord for me." She added that she had died that very same night that he had last seen her; she had traveled in one hour the distance that it took Zosimas twenty days to cover on foot.

After praying and weeping for a time, Zosimas said to himself, "It is time for you to do what you have been asked. But how shall you, miserable man, dig a grave with no instrument in your hands?" He found a stick and tried to dig with it, but the dry earth was too hard. He grew tired and covered with sweat. Then, looking up, he was terrified to see an immense lion standing near her feet. He recalled that Mary had said that, in all her years in the desert, she had never seen a living creature. Yet the lion came toward him as if it were a housecat, "expressing affection by every movement he made."

Zosimas spoke to the lion: "The great saint said her body was to be buried, but I am old and have not the strength to dig a grave without a spade, and it would take too long to go get one. Can you carry out the work with your claws? Then we can commit to the earth the mortal tabernacle of the saint." As he spoke, the lion began to dig a hole deep enough to bury her body.

Zosimas laid the body in the grave, "naked as it was before, not covered by anything but the tattered cloak that had been thrown to her by Zosimas." The lion then returned to the depths of the desert "just like a lamb," and Zosimas went back to his monastery. There he told the brothers the story of St. Mary, and "all wondered hearing the miracles of God, and with fear and love they celebrated the memory of the saint." Abbot John did indeed find certain things in the monastery that needed correction, "so that not a single word of the saint proved fruitless and without reason." Zosimas spent the rest of his life in the monastery, living to be almost a hundred years old.

"The monks kept this tradition without writing it down, bringing it to the notice of all who wished to listen. But I, as soon as I heard it, wrote it down. . . . May God, who works amazing miracles and generously bestows gifts on those who turn to Him with faith, reward those who seek light for themselves in this story, who hear, read, and are zealous to write it, and may He grant them the lot of blessed Mary, together with all those who have pleased God by their thoughts and labors from the beginning of the ages."

Acknowledgments

This English translation of The Canon of St. Andrew is reproduced here with the kind permission of Bishop Kallistos Ware of Diokleia, and the Orthodox Monastery of the Veil of the Mother of God in Bussy en Othe, France.

The text, along with other services of Great Lent, may be found in *"The Lenten Triodion,"* translated by Mother Mary and Bishop Kallistos Ware, published by St. Tikhon's Seminary Press.

www.stots.edu

The Canticle of Habbakuk is reprinted with the kind permission of Holy Transfiguration Monastery of Brookline, MA, and found in their book, *"The Psalter According to the Seventy."* It is a translation of the Psalms from the Septuagint, together with the Nine Biblical Odes.

www.thehtm.org

About Paraclete Press

WHO WE ARE

Paraclete Press is an ecumenical publisher of books on Christian spirituality for people of all denominations and backgrounds.

We publish books that represent the wide spectrum of Christian belief and practice—Catholic, Orthodox, and Protestant.

We market our books primarily through booksellers; we are what is called a "trade" publisher, which means that we like it best when readers buy our books from booksellers, our partners in successfully reaching as wide an audience as possible.

We are uniquely positioned in the marketplace without connection to a large corporation or conglomerate and with informal relationships to many branches and denominations of faith, rather than a formal relationship to any single one. We focus on publishing a diversity of thoughts and perspectives—the fruit of our diversity as a company.

WHAT WE ARE DOING

Paraclete Press is publishing books that show the diversity and depth of what it means to be Christian. We publish books that reflect the Christian experience across many cultures, time periods, and houses of worship.

We publish books about spiritual practice, history, ideas, customs, and rituals, and books that nourish the vibrant life of the church.

We have several different series of books within Paraclete Press, including the bestselling Living Library series of modernized classic texts, A Voice from the Monastery—giving voice to men and women monastics on what it means to live a spiritual life today, and Many Mansions—for exploring the riches of the world's religious traditions and discovering how other faiths inform Christian thought and practice.

Learn more about us at our web site:
www.paracletepress.com, or call us toll-free at
1-800-451-5006.

Also Available from Paraclete Press

The Illumined Heart
The Ancient Christian Path of Transformation
Frederica Mathewes-Green
ISBN: 1-55725-286-6
112 pages
$13.95, Hardcover

Why are Christians today so indistinguishable from everyone else? Why don't they stand out in virtue and joy? How is it that the early saints could seemingly fast valiantly, pray constantly, and love others consistently? Drawing on Christian writings throughout the early centuries, Frederica Mathewes-Green illuminates the ancient, trans-cultural faith of the early church and suggests how it can illuminate our lives today.

"Breathtakingly countercultural, and worth more to the honest seeker than shelves of what passes for practical spirituality these day . . . ."—*New York Post*

The Open Door
Entering the Sanctuary of Icons and Prayer
Frederica Mathewes-Green
ISBN: 1-55725-341-2
165 pages
$16.95, Hardcover

With warmth and insight, Mathewes-Green welcomes you into an imaginary Orthodox church to view twelve of the world's most famous icons throughout the church year. Includes full-color illustrations, stories of the saints, and prayers appointed for saints' special days.

Available from most booksellers or through Paraclete Press
www.paracletepress.com
1-800-451-5006
Try your local bookstore first.